Workplace Violence:
Before, During, and After

Sandra L. Lang

INTERNATIONAL
Advancing Security Worldwide™

To Floyd, Paul, and Ralph Taylor.

In loving memory of Ursula McRae.

TABLE OF CONTENTS

Foreword ix

Preface xi

Introduction xiii

Part One Aspects of Workplace Violence 1

    Chapter One   Introduction to Violence in the Workplace 3
    High-Risk Workplaces and Occupations 5
    The Statistics 8
    Normal Versus Abnormal Behavior 9

    Chapter Two   Forms of Violence 13
    Motivations for Violence 13
    Internal Crimes Against the Company 17
    Drug Abuse in the Workplace 18
    Domestic Violence in the Workplace 27
    Stalking 31

    Chapter Three   The Violent Person 37
    Profiles of the Violent Person 37
    Warning Signs of Violent Behavior 38
    Threats 40
    History of Violence 41
    History of Failed Relationships 41
    Distrust and Suspicion 42
    Unusual Claims 43
    Alcohol or Drug Abuse 43
    Ownership of Weapons 44
    Fascination with Weapons 45
    Fascination with Workplace Violence 46
    History of Harassment or Intimidation 46

Part Two Before Workplace Violence Occurs 49

Chapter Four   Employment Conditions and Violence 51
Ingredients for a Volatile Workplace 51
Corporate Policies and Procedures 55
Legal Aspects of a Secure Work Environment 57

Chapter Five   Education and Training 59
Employee Education 59
Manager and Supervisor Training 61
Crisis Intervention Team Training 62

Chapter Six   Policies and Procedures 65
Hiring 65
The Application Form and Resume 68
The Interview 70
The Background Check 72
Termination 73
Employee-Assistance Programs (EAPs) 77
Intervention and Action Plans 84
Security Procedures 90
Access Control 93
Physical Security 96
Security Management 98
Training 98

Part Three During Workplace Violence 101

Chapter Seven   Threatening Behavior 103
Dealing with Aggressive or Intimidating Behavior 104
Signs of Potentially Violent Behavior 109

Chapter Eight   Violent Behavior 113
Fight or Flight 118
Key Elements of Robbery 123
Robbery Deterrence 126
Surviving a Robbery 127
Responsibilities During a Robbery 128
Responsibilities After a Robbery 129
Duress Alarms 131

Part Four After Workplace Violence Has Occurred 133

Chapter Nine   Managing the Crisis 135
    Post-Incident Planning 135
    Media Coverage 137
    Post-Traumatic Stress 143

Part Five The California Occupational Safety and Health
        Administration's Model Program 151

Chapter Ten   The California Occupational Safety and Health
                Administration Addresses Workplace Violence 153
    Things to Come 154
    Who Should Use this Model Program? 155
    Workplace Violence in California 156
    Injury and Illness Prevention Program for Workplace Security . 158
    Responsibility 159
    Compliance 159
    Communication 160
    Hazard Assessment 161
    Incident Investigations 164
    Hazard Correction 165
    Training and Instruction 167

Conclusion 171

Index 173

About the Author 183

On October 29, 2002, Robert Stewart Flores, Jr., a 41-year-old Gulf War veteran and struggling student at the University of Arizona's College of Nursing, brought five guns and 200 rounds of ammunition to campus. He used at least one of the guns to shoot and kill three professors, sending the entire student body fleeing in panic and creating chaos and havoc. He then used the gun to kill himself. Could action have been taken that would have prevented this tragedy? Were there any telltale signs that could have alerted college officials of a possible threat of violence? Students described Flores as aggressive and obnoxious towards other students, and he often tangled with instructors. Just a year earlier he had openly bragged that he had obtained a concealed weapons permit. In April 2001, Flores had conveyed to college staff that he was depressed. There seems to have been numerous warning signs present that could have alerted staff to the potential threat.

Not all potential threats are so easily recognizable, however. Just a day later, on October 30, 2002, an unknown assailant shot and killed two women employees of a Dollar General Store in Deltona, Florida, during an apparent robbery. The act was senseless—as mostly all acts of workplace violence are. These are just two instances of violence in the workplace that I touched upon. The sad truth is that they occur all too often in our society, and no institution is exempt. Schools, banks, restaurants, post offices, manufacturing plants, and convenience stores—just to name a few—have all been targets of workplace violence. A 2002 survey conducted by Pinkerton ranked workplace violence as the Number One out of the Top 23 security concerns to corporate America. In fact, previous surveys conducted by Pinkerton have ranked it as the Number One threat yearly since 1997.

In this book, Sandra Lanier offers practical guidance on strategies to mitigate potential workplace violence. Specifically, Ms. Lanier describes the behavioral signs of potential problem employees and offers guidance on how to handle situations involving potential workplace violence. This book is an excellent resource guide and should be in the reference libraries of all security and human resource professionals. Two thumbs up!

Bruce C. List, CPI, CFE
Director of Enterprise Security
Williams

June 18, 1991, was, in many ways, a very significant day for me. It was on this day that I reported to work in my new position as Security Coordinator for a Fortune 500 company located in Iowa. After working my way up through the ranks in security positions and completing my college degree, I felt very positive about my professional future. There were about eight hundred people employed at this office—and I knew most of them by name.

On that day, I proudly set up my new office and accepted the congratulations of my coworkers. All was going well until I received a fateful phone call. A gunman had walked into an affiliate office in Jacksonville, Florida, and embarked on a bloody rampage. I would not understand the full significance of that telephone call for a long time to come.

Why had this happened? It turned out that the assailant's car had been repossessed earlier. He was late making his car payments and upset that the finance company had taken this action. He killed eight people and wounded five more. This tragedy made front-page headlines across the United States and sent shock waves across the country.

Even though the rampage took place over a thousand miles away and I did not personally know any of the people involved, the tragedy struck home. Employees at the office where I worked were grief-stricken for people they had never met. Listening to the gruesome details of the incident was painful. Employees feared for their own safety, and many no longer felt safe in the workplace. Employees immediately became extremely concerned about building security. They wanted guaranteed protection, and they wanted it immediately.

A group of employees demanded that metal detectors be installed at every door, that the reception area be contained in bulletproof glass, and that visitors, customers, and family members be searched for weapons as they entered the facility. Employees stopped using their last names in correspondences and on the telephone in an effort to protect their privacy.

When I got home that evening, I received numerous telephone calls, only one of which I remember with great detail. The call came from Jacksonville, Florida, where the killings had taken place. Because Jacksonville is a large town with thousands of offices and buildings, I had not made any connection between my family members who lived in Jacksonville and the murders that had taken place there. A telephone call from my twin sister, Deb, changed that and brought the shootings to a personal level. Deb had been working just a few blocks away at a video rental store when the shooting took place. Deb told me about the murders and the mass hysteria that had seized the town and the fear of all people near the shootings. She told me about rumors of the gunman being in the shopping plaza where she worked and locking all the customers in the store. She told me about trying to find the safest place in the store for customers to hide in case the gunman forced his way into the store.

This tragedy took eight lives. It robbed many people of their children, parents, siblings, and friends. It raised my awareness of the growing epidemic of workplace violence, and compelled me to write this book. Several years later, the brother of the gunman in the Jacksonville rampage beat a helpless elderly female clerk severely. She later died of her injuries. This clerk worked for my husband's company. We have both had employees killed by the same family in Jacksonville.

You cannot escape the responsibility of tomorrow by evading it today.

-Abraham Lincoln

On Monday, June 20, 1994, Dean Mellberg, recently discharged from the U.S. Air force for emotional problems, left his hotel room and sat quietly on a curb waiting for a taxi. Next to Mellberg was a large gym bag. The taxi took Mellberg ten miles to the Fairchild Air Force Hospital in Spokane, Washington. Once there, Mellberg began a violent and bloody rampage that took him and his Chinese-made MAK-90 down corridors, into specific offices, into the hospital cafeteria, and eventually out onto the hospital lawn.

The massacre ended when a military policeman on a bicycle shot and killed Mellberg. The death toll in the incident was five, with twenty-three others injured. Among those killed was Major Thomas Brigham, the psychiatrist who, with other mental health professionals, recommended that Mellberg be discharged. An eight-year-old girl sitting in the hospital cafeteria was also killed. The next day, eight victims remained in critical condition, including a four-year-old boy and a five-year-old girl.

Most of the people injured or killed at the air force hospital never met Mellberg. They were family members of military personnel stationed at the base, and it was just by chance that they happened to be at the hospital at the time of the shooting.

The trauma and tragedy unfolded the next day in front-page headlines across America. Millions of people read the articles or saw the news on television. The reports continued for some time, as the details of the killing spree became known and countless questions were answered.

As employees and employers, we have our own questions, which typically go unanswered. Probably the most common question is, "Why did this happen?" Other questions include, "Am I, or my company, at risk for this type of tragedy?" "What can be done?" "How can I tell if an employee in my firm is at the point of believing that violence is the answer?"

The truth is that there are no perfect, clear-cut answers. There are, however, specific indicators of potentially violent incidents, and there are established guidelines for protecting employees, customers, and organizations. That information is contained in this book.

Today, workplace intimidation, threats, physical assault, and homicide are issues that every business and worker must address. Incidents of violence in the workplace have increased so dramatically that the Centers for Disease Control and Prevention now considers occupational violence to be a serious public health problem.[1]

In December 2001, the U.S. Department of Justice issued a report that estimated between 1993 and 1999, an average of 1.7 million violent acts were committed against persons age 12 and older who were at work or on duty per year.[2] The days when "ignorance is bliss" are gone forever. The September 11 tragedy further increased our awareness that personal safety is now something we cannot take for granted. The increased threat of violence in organizations has challenged human resource managers, safety managers, and security managers to identify, examine, and eradicate the risks that their organizations face. The managers must now implement measures to prevent bloodshed in their workplaces. Meanwhile, newspaper headlines all across the United States continue to relate stories of fatal robberies, bombings, and murderous former employees.

The legal and social environments in which businesses operate have changed drastically over the past few years. The Occupational Safety and Health Administration (OSHA) has begun to cite employers who have not adequately addressed and dealt with threats of violence or harassment issues with costly fines. Companies and individuals can be held legally and criminally liable for failing to provide a safe and secure work environment. Lately, I've heard radio advertisements for attorneys looking to represent people injured as a result of inadequate security standards. Case law has awarded multimillion-dollar settlements to victims and their families when companies failed to provide security for their employees. The direction of the courts is clear: companies must address workplace security issues now or pay severely later.

The prevention of aggressive and violent behavior is not a simple matter. Violence in the workplace is not committed by a specific category of people. Those who commit violence include employees (former and current), their friends and family members, customers, vendors, felons, and other criminals including robbers.

Violence is possible in every type of workplace. The nature of and motivation for the violence are often directly related to the establishment's characteristics and the services offered. For example, police officers have the highest rate of occupational homicide.

Retail trade and services have a higher rate of robbery. When the likelihood of a robbery is reduced, the overall likelihood of occupational homicide is also reduced.

Researchers and professional security writers have focused on using behavioral red flags, warning signs, and generic profiles to identify potential employee offenders. Researchers have devised a profile for the "typical" offender. However, caution must be exercised when using this profile. Those who typecast certain employees may overlook others who harbor a propensity for violence without fitting the profile.

To understand the perspective of the potential offender, we must first understand human behavior as it relates to the relationship between individuals and their work. Social and economic considerations have played an important role in the increase of violence in the workplace. It may be that, in our culture, workplace violence is more acceptable than it was twenty years ago, or perhaps after reading about violence almost every day, we have become desensitized to it. Perhaps the media attention tied to workplace violence has actually encouraged offenders to get their "fifteen minutes of fame." I certainly believe this is a significant factor contributing to the increase in school violence.

Looking beyond the individual, businesses must examine themselves to identify any factors that make their workplaces conducive to violence. Company policies and procedures, security measures, hiring practices, disciplinary actions, and the effectiveness of employee-assistance programs (EAPs) must be measured.

The thoroughness of a company's planning can determine its ability to successfully cope with a violent incident. Acts of violence committed in the workplace can vary greatly in both their severity and impact on the organization. The effects can last from days to years. The biggest impact is the anguish the surviving employees and the victims' families are left to deal with. In some cases, counseling by mental health professionals can last for years, and some victims never fully regain their previous level of mental health and well-being.

Not every company has the resources available to provide a full-time, on-site security staff. The next best thing is to examine how the company can make the most of the resources it already has. Many options are available that do not cost tremendous amounts of money. The information in this book will assist small business owners lacking the resources of large corporations.

Written policies and procedures can help companies deter violence. A written recovery strategy can help companies identify, evaluate, control, and resolve potentially volatile situations when they arise. The time spent today on planning may later determine the extent of the effects of violence on the business, its employees and customers, and the community.

REFERENCES

1. U.S Department of Health and Human Services, Centers for Disease Control and Prevention, *Alert: Request for Assistance in Preventing Homicides in the Workplace* (Washington D.C.: U.S. Government Printing Office, 1993.)

2. Bureau of Justice Statistics, Special Report. *Violence in the Workplace 1993-99.* (Washington D.C.: U.S. Government Printing Office, December 2001), page 1.

PART ONE
ASPECTS OF WORKPLACE VIOLENCE

CHAPTER ONE
INTRODUCTION TO VIOLENCE IN THE WORKPLACE

Times are changing. When we look at the history of the United States, it's readily apparent that more changes have occurred in the past thirty years than in the previous two hundred years. In the past thirty years we have sent humans to the moon, developed airplanes capable of sending hundreds of people thousands of miles in a few short hours, and invented methods of instant communication via satellites, fax machines, the Internet, and cell phones. On a more personal level, think of the difference between the toys you played with as a child and the toys your children or grandchildren are playing with today. Thanks to technology, dolls are capable of talking back and developing interactive stories. This past Christmas, I walked into my sister's house, looked at the television, and asked which football teams were playing only to discover it was a computer game and not a broadcast.

The effect of all these changes is phenomenal. To put it bluntly, we are not the same society we were ten or twenty years ago. These rapid changes have affected the very fabric of our lives in both positive and negative ways.

For example, one benefit of rapid communications is faster access to information and news. We can sit in our easy chairs and watch the Olympics live, cheering with the rest of the nation as our proud athletes compete for world recognition and honors. Millions of people watched in astonishment as the Berlin Wall fell, witnessing the effect this had on other people thousands of miles away. Millions of people, including myself, watched in disbelief and horror as terrorists flew a plane into the second tower of the World Trade Center on live television.

Another effect of recent changes is having our parents, children, siblings, and other family members move to other parts of the country or world. With these changes, little of the "Leave It to Beaver" family atmosphere remains. Our natural family support groups have diminished. The divorce rate per 1,000 married women increased from 9.3 in 1955 to 21.2 in 1992. People today often feel alone and isolated from the rest of the world. Many people don't know their neighbors' names and don't really care about them as long as they don't have a dog that barks at

3

three o'clock in the morning. Crime rates have increased noticeably as well. According to the Bureau of Justice Statistics workplace violence accounted for 18 percent of all violent crime between 1993 and 1999 in the United States.[1]

Both positive and negative changes have also occurred in the workforce. On the positive side, more managerial classes are offered today and we are slowly moving away from an authoritarian management style toward focused work groups and team-based models. Ball-and-chain management styles are being replaced with team concepts, and work and family issues are finally being addressed. Few employee assistance programs existed twenty years ago, but now they play an integral role in many larger corporations. Companies are beginning to recognize the value of their employees as part of their real assets. The Americans with Disabilities Act (ADA) now requires employers to make modifications or reasonable accommodations for the special needs of their employees.

On the negative side, layoffs are an everyday occurrence. Call it "downsizing" or "rightsizing" or whichever term you like—the results are the same. People are losing their jobs by the thousands. The majority of the workers in the United States who have not lost their jobs due to a layoff know family members or close friends who have. Even those who are not directly affected still experience the indirect effects of layoffs or job terminations. Relocation to other cities for other jobs distances people from family members and friends. This erodes a person's support network.

Workers see their friends and families struggle to make ends meet as they slowly sell off possessions to avoid losing their homes. Savings accounts that took a lifetime to build up are quickly spent. They can't even hope to replace their retirement or kids' college money that took years of struggling to acquire. Somewhere in the back of most people's minds is the fear that it could happen to them. This is true for the majority of workers in the United States. Most of us can become a statistic in the blink of an eye; and it can happen today or tomorrow. Life has indeed changed.

Twenty years ago, a job loss was a traumatic event for most people. The newly unemployed might spend a day or two grieving or brooding over the job loss and then get busy filling out applications with potential employers. After a day, a week, or a month, they usually found a comparable job at a comparable wage with comparable benefits. Life went on.

Today's job market does not have the same guarantees. It is more competitive than ever before. There are often fifty to 250 applicants for every "good" job available. The jobs that are readily available are often part-time or temporary jobs that pay close to minimum wage and offer few or no benefits. These types of positions usually seem demeaning to workers who are accustomed to a wage of fifteen dollars per hour and a cafeteria-style benefits plan. They believe that these types of jobs are more suitable for kids paying their way through college than for wage earners trying to support a family. In addition, automation is replacing manual labor. Job loss and the threat of job loss are just two of the reasons for the alarming increase in workplace violence.

HIGH-RISK WORKPLACES AND OCCUPATIONS

Given the ongoing publicity, it may seen surprising that the U.S. Postal Service does not have the highest rate of workplace homicide. In fact, the U.S. Postal Service does not even make the top-ten list. Although post office murders attract a great deal of media attention, the Postal Service has a lower homicide rate than the national average. Media sensationalism contributes to the "going postal" hysteria associated with workplace violence.

When the National Institute for Occupational Safety and Health (NIOSH) calculates the incident rates for workplaces, the formula used is based on the number of homicides per one hundred thousand workers. Workplaces are defined according to the *Standard Industry Classification (SIC) Manual.* The simple formula is as follows: Number of homicides per SIC Code ÷ number of employees per SIC code.

The larger the number of employees, the lower the ratio of employees to homicides. Because the U.S. Postal Service is the third largest employer in the United States, the ratio is likely to be lower.

The occupations with the highest rates of occupational violence during 1993-1999, according to the 1999 National Census of Fatal Occupational Injuries, are listed in Table 1-1.

Table 1-1
Rates of Victimization in the Workplace, by Occupational Field[1]

	1993	1994	1995	1996	1997	1998	1999
Medical	20.3	16.7	16	11.8	8.4	9.2	10
Mental Health	64.4	63.7	56.7	63.9	39.7	49.3	46.1
Teaching	25.8	19.3	15.4	16.6	14.9	18.9	12.4
Law Enforcement	163.1	156.4	157.2	125.9	122	88.5	74.1
Retail Sales	21.9	22.8	22.2	20.4	20.5	16.2	14.1
Transportation	20.6	24.1	13.8	12.6	15.4	18.3	8.4
Other	8.1	9.6	7.4	7.3	5.1	6.6	5.3

Table 1-2 shows the homicide rates for selected industries between 1994 and 1999. There were 5,260 recorded workplace homicides during the six years.

Table 1-2
Workplace Homicides for Selected Industries During 1994-1999[2]

Workplace	Number of Homicides					
	1994	1995	1996	1997	1998	1999
Total Homicides	1,080	1,034	927	860	714	645
Retail Trade	530	422	437	395	286	260
Grocery Stores	196	152	146	141	95	76
Eating and Drinking Establishments	135	121	135	109	69	94
Gasoline Service Stations	41	36	23	34	24	17
Taxicab	87	68	50	74	48	51
Detective and Armored Car Services	49	27	29	21	18	17
Police Protection	65	61	45	61	50	41

The U.S. Department of Justice completed a victimization survey in December 2001, that categorized victimization by type of crime. The results of that survey are shown in Table 1.3. Another survey conducted by the U.S. Department of Justice shows the national crime victimization from 1973-2000. Those survey results are shown in Table 1-4. The tables show that over 75 percent of workplace violence incidents are categorized as simple assault with over 1.3 million victims per year.

Table 1.3
Average Annual Number, Rate, and Percent of Workplace Victimization by Type of Crime, 1993–1999[3]

Crime Category	Rate per 1,000 Persons in the Workforce	Average Annual Workplace Victimization	Percent of Workplace Victimization
All Violent Crime	12.5	1,744,300	100%
Homicide	0.01	900	0.01
Rape/Sexual Assault	0.03	36,500	2.1
Robbery	0.05	70,100	4
Aggravated Assault	2.3	325,000	18.6
Simple Assault	9.4	1,311,700	75.2

Table 1-4
National Crime Victimization Survey of Violent Crime Trends, 1973-2000[4]

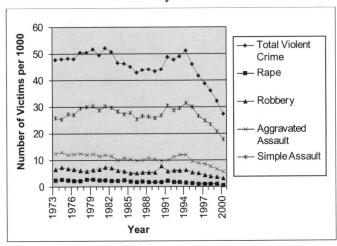

The following risk factors are associated with workplace violence:

- Exchanging money

- Working alone at night and during early morning hours

- Having money, valued items, jewelry, or other items that are easily exchanged for cash

- Performing public safety functions in the community

- Working with patients, clients or customers known to have, or suspected of having, a history of violence

- Working with employees with a history of assaults, or who exhibit belligerent, intimidating, or threatening behavior toward others.

THE STATISTICS

Statistics can be fascinating. They are available on almost every subject you can imagine. Whether you are interested in the number of births in your county or the number of fish caught in a local pond in 1978, you can probably find the answer buried in your library or on the Internet somewhere. Statistical analysis is a combination of art and science. Much of the validity of the statistics depends on the people conducting the research

Knowing the numbers alone will not stop or prevent violence; the numbers serve only as a means of looking at the past and predicting future events in a given set of circumstances. The tables and figures in this chapter are valuable in that they show crime trends based on various factors.

To gain insight into the extent of workplace violence, the statistics need to be compared to crime in the United States as a whole. A comparison of the increase in violent acts in general and the increase in violent acts in the workplace shows that incidents of workplace violence are increasing more rapidly that most other crimes. Crime trend data reveal a comprehensive scope of workplace violence.

Crime in the United States is undoubtedly on the rise. According to the "crime clocks" formulated by the *Uniform Crime Reports*, in 1962, a forcible rape was committed every thirty-two minutes in the United States; in 1992, a forcible rape was committed every five minutes.

According to the Uniform Crime Reports, the incidence of murder has increased 23 percent from 1983 to 1992. Total violent crimes (murder, forcible rape, robbery, and aggravated assault) climbed 53.6 percent during the same period. Occupational homicide is growing at a much faster rate than other categories of murder. Because record keeping on occupational homicides is relatively new, few actual figures are available, and the increase can only be estimated. For California, there was a 22.6 percent increase in occupation homicides in just one year (1992-1993).

According to the 1993 Census of Fatal Occupational Injuries, 1,063 people died on the job as a result of work-related homicides. The majority of these homicides occurred during a robbery or other crime. Robberies and miscellaneous crimes accounted for 793 (75 percent) of the 1,063 occupational deaths in 1993. The next largest category of job-related homicides was homicides committed by work-related associates —106 (10 percent) of the deaths. Of these, 59 occurred at the hands of a current or former worker. In the rest of the work-related homicides, customers or clients committed 43 murders. Personal acquaintances accounted for 4 percent of occupational homicides; and security officers, 5 percent. The motives involved in the remaining 4 work-related homicides were not specified. The number of murders committed by work associates could easily be twice as high; many of these crimes may have been reported and recorded as other criminal acts. For example, if one employee kills another employee outside of the work environment, the murder might not be classified as a work-related homicide.

NORMAL VERSUS ABNORMAL BEHAVIOR

Why do we act the way we do in a given set of circumstances? Chances are, at one time or another, we've all acted in a way that surprised even ourselves. There are times when "the devil made me do it" is our only defense. What makes us act the way we do?

Most of the time, we try to act like the responsible, caring people that we want to be. We try to treat our friends well; otherwise they wouldn't be our friends. We love our spouses, try to get along with our coworkers, attend services at a house of worship, sometimes give time and money to charities, and refrain from beating the dog.

Once in awhile, though, we argue with our spouse, clash with the boss, and yell at the dog. We know we're not perfect, but we like to think we're good people. We like to think the same of friends and family.

Then as we sit down to watch the evening news, we see the murder trial of a mother who murdered her children by drowning them in a bathtub. Everybody who listens to the gruesome details is emotionally affected. People worry because they fear for their own children; they turn away in disgust. We ask ourselves how this could happen and what kind of person this mother is. Advocates for the death penalty appear to be everywhere.

The news anchor the opens the next segment with video from the latest court developments in another murder trial. The story after that gives the details of a gang-related drive-by shooting in which three kids were killed. The next report is about a big drug bust. The following piece covers the overcrowding at the local jail. The kind feelings we had half an hour ago give way to the suspicion that we are stuck in the middle of a very sick society. Add to the mixture the insanity of the September 11th disaster and a bank robbery ending with five murders in Norfolk, Nebraska, and abnormal and demented behavior seems to be everywhere.

We question how people can commit such acts of violence against others. We know that sooner or later these crimes will spread from other people's neighborhoods into our own. We consider how long it will be before an armed desperado comes into our office, our home, our life and opens fire. We dread the thought of our own family members and friends becoming victims.

Again, we wonder what it is that makes a person act in a certain way. Once, a security officer told me that everybody out there is fighting his or her own form of mental illness and is one step away from falling from social graces. In the years since, I have reflected on that thought numerous times. I think the statement was more perceptive than even the security officer intended. I suspect each of us has ghosts in our closest and feelings we would never dare share with others. Maybe understanding our own feelings and fears, and their origins, can help us comprehend the behavior of others. By looking at the environment in which we operate, we can see ways that we can improve society.

Even on the most difficult day, though, few of us would consider using violence as the means to an end. Not all people affected by stress will turn to violence and not all forms of mental illness lead to violence. *Abnormal behavior* is a broad term that can describe conditions related to mental illness, alcohol intoxication, drug-induced impairments, and stress related disorders. This is only a partial list of the causes of abnormal behavior.

Due to diversity among people's cultures, it's difficult to describe what might be considered abnormal behavior. In one set of circumstances, a certain behavior may be totally appropriate, whereas the same actions would be considered abnormal elsewhere.

One way to think about normal versus abnormal behavior is to think about what the reasonable person might expect in a particular set of circumstances. For the most part, this parallels the way our judicial system works in the United States. When trying to figure out if an employee's behavior would be considered normal, evaluate what the reasonable person would do. Keep in mind that the reasonable person is someone who is both like and unlike the typical manager, supervisor, or employee. The reasonable person may not have the same heritage, background, values, or goals as every other person. What may seem totally inconceivable to one person may seem perfectly normal to another. Diversity exists in the workplace, and the amount of diversity will grow and continue to be a powerful characteristic of the workplace in the future.

Imagine for a moment that all of your employees are invited to a company-sponsored picnic. Each employee is to bring a side dish to accompany the hotdogs and hamburgers supplied by the company. Depending on the diversity of the workplace, you might expect to see all kinds of ethnic food. What about the employee who brings a steaming platter of Alpo? Most people would consider this abnormal.

Now consider how the reasonable person would respond to conflict in the workplace. With this example, it might be harder to give an exact answer because people react differently. When a conflict arises in the workplace, one person might want to cry, another might withdraw socially, and yet another might quit. Under any set of circumstances, it would not be normal to threaten violence against oneself or another. This behavior is simply not appropriate in the workplace. In this day and age, it would not be reasonable to think that violence, in any form, should be used when dealing with conflict or stress. Employees who do use threatening, intimidating or violent actions to "win" need to be dealt with. Returning to the Alpo example earlier, one of the bloodiest fights I've ever heard about involved how to properly cook grits. In June of 2001, a man was arrested for assaulting the Cookie Monster after the Cookie Monster allegedly refused to pose with his daughter. If the Cookie Monster is not safe from workplace violence, then I suppose very few of us are.

REFERENCES

1. U.S. Department of Justice/Bureau of Labor Statistics, Special Report. *Violence in the Workplace 1993-99.* (Washington D.C.: U.S. Government Printing Office, December 2001), p. 3.

2. Ibid., p. 4.

3. Ibid., p. 2.

4. Ibid., p. 2.

When business owners and managers think about violence in the work-place, they often visualize a former employee brandishing a handgun. This type of workplace violence represents only a small percentage of actual cases. Robberies, assaults, rapes, and verbal abuse occur much more frequently. On any given day in the United States, hundreds of people become the victims of less publicized incidents of workplace violence.

According to a survey conducted by the Society of Human Resource Managers (SHRM) in 1993, 44 percent of the companies surveyed re-ported that acts of violence had occurred in the workplace that year; 29.6 percent reported three to five incidents of violence in the work-place during the past five years.[1]

Violent crimes are committed against employees for a variety of rea-sons. Examining the motivations for violence in the workplace can indicate the types of violence that might affect various occupations; in-vestigating the victim/offender relationship can help determine which employees are at risk.

MOTIVATIONS FOR VIOLENCE

In 1994, the California Division of Occupational Safety and Health Ad-ministration (CAL/OSHA) issued a set of guidelines intended to reduce incidents of workplace violence.[2] It is widely believed that the federal Occupational Safety and Health Administration will mirror these guide-lines when developing national standards. (CAL/OSHA's Guidelines are covered in Chapter 10.)

In the guidelines, violent incidents in the workplace are divided into three types of events. (See the box CAL/OSHA's Major Types of Work-place Violence".) These categories are based on the relationship, if any, of the offender to the victim or the workplace where the crime occurred. CAL/OSHA recommends specific security measures to guard against each type of violence.

CAL/OSHA's Major Types of Workplace Violence

Type I

The offender does not have a legitimate relationship with the business or its employees. Robbery is often the motive. This category represents the majority of cases of workplace violence. Typical victims include the following:·

- Convenience and liquor store employees

- Taxicab drivers

- Restaurant and grocery store employees

- Hotel and motel clerks

Type II

The victim is a service provider, and the assailant is a recipient of those services. The following are typical victims of this type of violence:

- Police and public safety professionals

- Medical care providers

- Social workers

- Attorneys and judges

Type III

The assailant has some sort of relationship with the business or an employee. Typical assailants in this type of violence include the following:

- Current or former employees

- Current or former friends of employees

- Relatives of employees

- Current or former customers

- Current or former vendors

In Type 1 incidents, the offender does not have a legitimate relationship with the employees or the business itself. The motive for this category is often robbery or another act of violence. This category represents the majority of workplace homicides that occur in California. In most of these incidents, the criminal enters a small retail establishment late at night with the intention of robbing the attendant. During the course of the robbery, the attendant—often the owner—is sometimes killed.

The following risk factors are often present during this type of incident:

• The business exchanges money with customers.

• Few employees are present at the time.

• The business operates at night or early in the morning.

• Employees have face-to-face contact with customers.

Businesses with the highest incident rate in the category include gas stations, convenience stores, liquor stores, and similar businesses. Security officers, janitorial staff, and taxi drivers killed while on duty are included in this category. Many of these incidents occur in an almost random fashion. The act of violence is often unpredictable and unforeseeable. Criminals most likely pick their targets based on which businesses are the most convenient or are the easiest to victimize. Employees who know what to look for have a much better opportunity of predicting potentially violent or threatening situations.

The victims of Type II incidents are service providers. While fulfilling their job-related responsibilities, they are victimized as a result of the service they provide. Police officers and others employed in law enforcement and corrections are prime candidates for violence directed toward them in the course of employment. Besides law enforcement and corrections, other occupations at risk for Type II violence include:

• Medical-care providers

• Mental-health providers

• Alcohol and drug treatment employees

• Correctional facility employees

• Social workers in almost every field

- Justice System employees, including judges and attorneys

- Other public safety officials

For workers who fit into Type II occupations, the threat of violence is almost a daily occurrence. According to CAL/OSHA, Type II violence is increasing. In terms of nonfatal injuries to workers, this category of violence may be the most widespread.

In Type III incidents, the assailant has some type of relationship with either an employee or the business. The assailant could be a current or former employee seeking revenge against another employee, a supervisor, a manager, or the establishment itself. The offender could be the current or former spouse, or lover of an employee. Other examples of crimes in this category include violent acts at the workplace in which the victim and the offender have a relationship external to the workplace. Stalking cases that end violently at the work site are classified as Type III incidents.

Occurrences of Type III violence typically attract a great deal of media attention. One reason for this might be that no matter who you are or where you work, you can't know with any degree of certainty if another employee is on the verge of committing a violent act at your workplace. People can readily see themselves as a potential victim. Employees can only speculate about the emotional well-being of coworkers and, in some case, their friends and families. Media coverage of these types of incidents has almost created a panic among employees. Hovering helicopters outside of evacuated buildings with SWAT team members brandishing high-powered rifles makes for intense news coverage, but also reminds people of their lack of immunity to violence in their workplaces.

Almost unheard of fifteen years ago, Type III incidents are increasing at an alarming rate. It's impossible to escape the stories of former employees and disgruntled workers returning to the work site in a violent manner. Murders within the U.S. Postal Service have made headlines from coast to coast. The American Dialect Society selected the phrase "going postal" as 1995's word of the year. Although Type III incidents might not cause the most occupational homicides, managers and supervisors would be extremely foolish to believe that such incidents could never happen at their work site. The good news is that managers and supervisors do have some control over the Type III incidents occurring at their workplaces.

Verbal abuse, assaults, and rapes occurring among coworkers are far more common than occupational homicides. Because these acts of violence are greatly unreported, the extent of the abuse can only be estimated. According to the National Crime Victimization Survey conducted by the Bureau of Justice Statistics in 2001, 18 percent of all violent crimes are work related. The Bureau estimates that 1,743,300 workers were assaulted (simple assault, aggravated assault, robbery and rape) while on duty on between 1993 and 1999.[3]

The relationships among coworkers and between management and employees can be instrumental in determining a particular business' risk of workplace violence. Training and education are key factors in preventing Type III incidents. Many preventative steps and security measures can be used to protect against each category of violence; they are covered in Chapter 6. The CAL/OSHA guidelines for preventing violence in the workplace are summarized in Chapter 10.

INTERNAL CRIMES AGAINST THE COMPANY

Violence can take many forms, each varying in intensity and potential destructive behavior. Whereas some acts of violence are committed against people, many other acts are committed against equipment, products, and information, to name just a few. Acts that the perpetrator might view as only mildly destructive can have extremely harmful effects on the company as a whole.

A few carefully placed keystrokes can severely damage the financial stability of almost any company. There is no "truth in posting" policy on the Internet. A motivated individual with a limited amount of knowledge and a few extra bucks can post a website publishing false or negative information about a company. Companies have been crippled and even closed by a disgruntled employee who seeks revenge for something as simple as the discontinuation of the annual Christmas bonus.

Sabotage that forces a business to close its doors obviously has far-reaching and devastating effects on employees, business owners (including stockholders, who may include the majority of employees), customers, and the community. Pharmaceutical companies that have experienced product tampering by employees have spent millions of dollars on tamper-proof containers, not to speak of the millions sunk into litigation and settlements. Depending on the extent of the damages done and the negative publicity, companies may never again regain customer confidence. Companies that have experienced the end result of sabotage can readily see why product information and service integrity is such a vital part of the overall company mission statement.

Destructive acts of violence by an employee or customer can start on a small scale; the damage is often blamed on carelessness, accidents, normal breakdown of equipment, or a host of other causes. The true origin of the damage is rarely determined. Supervisors and managers who are busy trying to meet production quotas or keep up with daily tasks might overlook the incident rather than spend countless hours conducting an investigation that they believe will most likely lead to a dead end. Employees who have a tendency to damage or destroy company property may begin to believe that if management overlooks their acts of destruction, they have a license to continue acting destructively.

DRUG ABUSE IN THE WORKPLACE

Abuse of legal and illegal drugs by employees both on and off the job is increasing. The implications of this increase are devastating to U.S. businesses. The costs associated with drug abuse are astonishing. According to the U.S. Department of Health and Human Services, which conducted an extensive study in the mid-eighties on the economic costs associated with alcohol and drug abuse and mental illness, alcohol abuse had an economic cost of $70.3 billion in 1985. The economic cost of drug abuse was estimated at $44.1 billion, and mental illness had an estimated $103.7 billion impact on the U.S. economy.[4]

In 1985, crimes associated with alcohol and drug abuse and mental illness resulted in prison sentences totaling an estimated 232,530 years. That's in one year alone! Using eighty as the average human life span, this equates to 2,907 lives wasted in one year alone.

The future trends of abuse are even grimmer when we consider that the high school students of today will be the workers of tomorrow. In a survey conducted of twelfth graders in 1993, 62.5 percent of the respondents reported having been drunk at some point in their life. An astonishing 72 percent reported using alcohol in the past thirty days. In the same study, 42.9 percent reported using illicit drugs, including marijuana, hallucinogens, cocaine, heroin, stimulants, barbiturates, and tranquilizers not prescribed by a doctor.[5] The majority of these twelfth graders have already entered the workforce. The graduating high school classes in the past decade are very familiar with drug and alcohol abuse among their friends and peers.

Clearly, drug and alcohol abuse are problems encountered at all workplaces throughout the United States. The abuse has become so widespread that supervisors are required to undergo training to detect symptoms and signs indicative of alcohol and drug abuse among employees who drive vehicles on the job. This law, the Omnibus Employee Testing Act, requires drivers to submit to an alcohol or controlled substance test when the employer has reasonable suspicion that the driver is in violation of alcohol or controlled substance regulations. The Omnibus Employee Testing Act states:

> Each employer shall ensure that persons designated to determine whether reasonable suspicion exists to require a driver to undergo testing receive at least 60 minutes of training on controlled substance use. The training shall cover physical, behavioral, speech and performance indicators of probable misuse and use of controlled substances.

The aim of the training is to give supervisors the tools they need to identify potential problem employees. Once an employee has been identified as a possible substance abuser, the supervisor has a responsibility to monitor job behavior and performance. The employer must require a driver to submit to alcohol or controlled substance testing when reasonable suspicion has been established. The employer must also require additional testing when the employee returns to work from a substance abuse program and periodically thereafter.

The intention of this law is to prevent employees who are misusing alcohol or controlled substances from injuring themselves or other people. The supervisor must also act in accordance with company policies regarding workplace safety and substance abuse.

Although not every company is subject to this regulation, training on drug abuse is a valuable tool for all supervisors, managers, and employees in the battle to curb workplace violence. According to a survey conducted by Northwestern National Life Insurance Company and published by *EAP Digest* in 1994, 59 percent of U.S. workers believe that alcohol and drug abuse is a factor in workplace violence.[6]

Employees who are abusing or misusing alcohol or controlled substances are more likely to have performance problems than their peers. Managers and supervisors need to know how to deal with abusers. Ignoring the behavioral or performance problems associated with the abuse will only postpone inevitable counseling or disciplinary actions. (See the box "Signs of Drug Misuse in the Workplace.") Because part of the employee's problem includes denial, the problem is likely to continue to grow without a third party, such as the employer, intervening.

> Employees with a drinking problem are absent 16 times more than the average employee, have an accident rate that is 4 times higher, use one-third more sickness benefits and have 5 times more compensation claims while on the job. Forty percent of industrial fatalities and 47 percent of industrial injuries can be traced to alcohol abuse.[7]

The supervisor who has reasonable cause to believe that an employee is either physically or mentally impaired as the result of substance abuse needs to respond in a manner that minimizes the potential danger associated with the impairment while maximizing the safety of others with whom the impaired employee may come into contact. Each company should have an alcohol and substance abuse policy that provides guidance and support to the supervisory and management staff. The policy should be clearly displayed and communicated to all employees when hired and at least annually thereafter.

Signs of Drug Misuse in the Workplace

Attendance

Tardiness arriving for work

Tardiness returning from lunch

Leaving the workplace

Frequent absences

Missed appointments

Absences from work

Quality of Work

Increased mistakes

Lack of attention/concentration

Difficulty recalling instructions

Missed deadlines

Productivity

Jobs take longer

Erratic/declining productivity

Wide swings in productivity

Assignment Changes

Requests for work with minimal supervision

Requests for work with other suspected substance abusers

Refusal of others to work with suspected abuser

Mood Changes

Unusual flare-ups or outbursts

Personality changes

Change in overall attitude

Overreaction to criticism

Blaming other for mistakes

Wide mood swings

Miscellaneous Signs

Secretive behavior

Numerous suspicious telephone calls or messages

Frequent trips to the rest room, locker, or other places away from the work site

Unreasonable or unexplained financial difficulties

Unreasonable or unexplained wealth

Constant sleepy appearance

Drug paraphernalia at the work site

Dramatic change in number or types of friends

Relationships

Difficulties with coworkers

Withdrawal from family

Loner behavior

Disruptive behavior

Overly critical of others

Association with known substance abusers

Injuries and Accidents

More frequent illnesses

Longer recovery from minor illnesses or accidents

Failure to use required safety equipment

Increase in workers' compensation claims

Appearance

Deterioration of overall health, hygiene, and habits

Rapid or extreme weight loss

Major changes in style of dress

Inappropriate wearing of sunglasses

Unusual efforts to hide arms with clothes or tattoos

Drug Symptoms

Cocaine

Possible effects: Nasal redness, runny nose, talkativeness, increased alertness, euphoria, loss of appetite, anxiety.

Noncocaine Stimulants

Possible effects: restlessness, talkativeness, dry mouth, body tremors, increased alertness, euphoria, insomnia, loss of appetite, anxiety.

Phencyclidine

Possible effects: blank stare, cyclic behavior, warm to the touch, perspiration, muscle rigidity, disorientation, repetitive speech, incomplete verbal responses, speech difficulty, noncommunicative, confusion, agitation, increased pain threshold, illusions, combative behavior.

Hallucinogens

Possible effects: dazed appearance, body tremors, hallucinations, perspiration, memory loss, poor perception of time and distance, lack of coordination, paranoia, muscle tension, hypersensitivity, nausea, disorientation, speech difficulty, flashbacks.

Cannabis

Possible effects: redness of the eyes, body tremors, marijuana debris in the mouth, odor of burnt marijuana, relaxed inhibitions, disorientation, increased appetite, impaired perception of time and distance, lack of attention, paranoia.

Inhalants

Possible effects: odor of the substance, substance on hands or face, confusion, disorientation, slurred speech, bloodshot, watery or inflamed eyes.

Depressants

Possible effects: drowsiness, lack of coordination, sluggishness, slurred speech, disorientation, drunken behavior.

Narcotics

Possible effects: droopy eyelids, drowsiness, extremely relaxed body composure, depressed reflexes, low and raspy speech, dry mouth, facial itching, euphoria, fresh puncture marks.

I interviewed Arlin Ciechanowski, a drug recognition expert (DRE), to gain a law enforcement perspective on drug abuse. Ciechanowski has spent most of his career trying to win the war against drugs. He obtained his master's degree in Criminal Justice Administration and has received extensive training through the Federal Bureau of Investigation in the area of drug detection and abuse. He now spends his days training other law enforcement officers on how to stay alive while doing their jobs. Part of Ciechanowski's training took him to the streets of Los Angeles, where knowing how to spot illicit drug use sometimes means the difference between going home at the end of the day and going to the morgue.

Ciechanowski is quick to point out that the people he deals with as a street cop are not typically the same ones a supervisor or manager deals with on the job. Many of his cases involve people whose addictions have already made it impossible for them to maintain any type of responsible employment.

Most addicts, Ciechanowski says, were at one time in the workforce before drugs became the ruling force in their lives. Eventually poor performance and absenteeism resulting from drug or alcohol abuse cost them their jobs. Education is a useful tool for managers and supervisors to help detect alcohol and drug abuse in the workplace. With training and assistance programs, there might be a chance to rehabilitate employees and help them straighten out their lives before they end up unemployable.

When asked why drug abuse is so prevalent in today's society, Ciechanowski says that for many kids in many cities, it is easier to be involved in drugs than not to be involved with them. "A fourteen-year-old can make five thousand dollars a week selling cocaine," he says. "Cocaine is more expensive than gold when compared ounce to ounce. With availability of money like that, there's a powerful motivation for kids to sell drugs."

Employers today must be concerned about drug abuse among juveniles because these kids will enter the workforce when they are older. Not only are kids becoming involved with hard-core drugs, but also they are experimenting with all sorts of other dangerous, and potentially fatal, drugs.

Ciechanowski points out that it isn't just young people doing drugs. "Sixty million prescriptions for tranquilizers are written during a typical year," he says. "While many of the people taking these tranquilizers are doing so legally, they are definitely showing up at their workstations with their ability to perform their jobs being severely impaired. Add to that the 20 percent of males, ages twenty-five to thirty-four who use marijuana at least once a month, and companies are facing a labor force that is making decisions on impaired abilities."

The first thing supervisors need to do if they suspect an employee may be under the influence of drugs or alcohol is remove the employee from areas that could be unsafe. The employee should not be allowed to operate a motor vehicle or any heavy equipment. Do not leave suspected abusers unattended; if their abilities are diminished, they may act in a manner that is dangerous to themselves or others.

When a drug overdose is suspected, emergency medical attention should be sought for the employee. Even if the employee refuses medical treatment from paramedics, an ambulance should be called. Remember that the employee's decision-making skills may be impaired as a result of the substance abuse.

Two or more employees should be assigned to watch the employee. Some drugs, such as angel dust and PCP, could compel the employee to have delusions and become combative. A person under the influence of PCP could fight a dozen people under the mistaken belief that he or she is in a life-threatening struggle. Some people also become combative under the influence of alcohol. At the first sign of combative behavior, call law enforcement officials. Certain drugs can produce violent behavior and, because of the impairment and the effects of the drugs, it is possible that the user will feel no pain at all. The lack of response to pain makes restraining the individual difficult or impossible.

The two people watching the employee should document all their observations regarding the employee. Having two similar reports of the incident provides stronger justification for intervention. When documenting the behavior and actions of an employee with drug- or alcohol-impaired abilities, record the company policy that is breached by the performance or behavior. For example, if the employee failed to wear required protective equipment, such as safety goggles, then the documentation should reflect not only the actions of the employee, but also the violation of the company policy regarding safety equipment.

If your company policy requires the suspected impaired employee to undergo testing at an off-site medical facility, have a security officer or manager accompany the employee in a taxicab. If left to take the taxi ride alone, the impaired employee could stop off at the corner convenience store and drink a six-pack of beer on the way. This would obviously lead to a positive test result; and with the driver as a witness to the drinking, the test results would have diminished meaning for the employer. You also don't want the impaired employee to re-direct the taxi driver to take the employee home or elsewhere.

Witnesses should document their observations regarding the employee's behavior. Statements made by the employee and the time, date, action, and location all need to be included in the report. The actions taken by management in response to the situation should also be recorded. If law enforcement officials are called in to respond to the situation, they should be asked to provide management with a copy of their report. With many law enforcement agencies, obtaining a copy of the report may take a few days. At least obtain a case number from the responding officer. Each of these reports should be placed in a separate file within the employee's personnel file. Later, if a lawsuit is brought against the company, the documentation will help defend the company's actions.

The supervisor should not attempt to counsel or discipline an impaired employee. The supervisor should also refrain from making moral judgments. An intoxicated employee is not in the frame of mind to comprehend the gravity of the situation. Give him or her time to recover from the effects of the substance. Discussions can take place at a later time.

When you do confront an employee, you should have written documentation of the incident and the breaches in company policy. Prepare, in advance, an action plan for the employee's improvement along with specific performance objectives. Supply the employee with the time frames for completing the performance objectives.

Do not try to diagnose or treat the employee's problem. Most supervisors do not have the training to deal with alcohol or drug problems. Instead, refer the individual to an employee-assistance program or to a counseling agency staffed with professionals trained in substance abuse. More information on counseling problem employees is provided in Chapter 6.

DOMESTIC VIOLENCE IN THE WORKPLACE

Domestic violence is an issue that every business should address. It is present everywhere, whether its signs are recognized or not. The damages caused by domestic violence can have a significant impact on a company's bottom line. The Bureau of National Affairs estimates that companies lose $3 to $5 billion each year as a result of domestic violence.[8] According to the 1999 Census of Fatal Occupational Injuries, five percent of work-related homicides stem from personal relationships.[9]

The job performance of employees who become involved in abusive relationships is negatively affected. Absenteeism, stress, and medical problems increase. Each of these problems carries a sizable price tag. The increased potential for internal acts of violence cannot be ignored either.

Statistics on the extent of domestic abuse in the United States vary. The American Medical Society estimates that almost four million women are victims of severe assaults by boyfriends and husbands each year. One woman in four is likely to be abused by a partner at some time in her life.[10]

According to another source, "even the minimum estimates indicate that at least two million women in the United States are severely assaulted (e.g., on an aggravated assault level) by a male partner during an average 12 month period. Researchers in the field agree that a more accurate national estimate would be a figure of four million women are severely assaulted by male partners annually, and an estimate of 40 percent of adult couples have experienced at least one aggressive incident in their current relationship."[11] Men are also the victims of assaults by both men and women. While this text focuses on female victims, the information is also pertinent to men involved in abusive relationships. This type of threat cannot be ignored.

Any police officer will tell you that a domestic dispute is one of the most dangerous and difficult calls to handle. The parties are typically very agitated and angry. To add further obstacles, often one or both people are highly intoxicated and their behavior is unpredictable. When police officers attempt to intervene, the parties can easily turn on them. If you accept the statistic of a 25 percent abuse rate, apply that figure to the number of female employees in your business. It almost seems inconceivable that 25 out of 100 female employees has been in, or is currently in, an abusive relationship. If your company has 1,000 female employees, then roughly 250 of those employees have faced domestic violence. These statistics clearly indicate that the potential for a violent incident occurring in your workplace is high.

The sad truth is that most people, at some time in their lives, experience a bad or failed relationship with a domestic partner, spouse, or lover. These failed relationships often involve many more people than the two that are facing the difficulties; children, parents, in-laws, neighbors, and friends are commonly involved in failing relationships. Often, other employees who are friends with the separating couple get involved in the breakup of a relationship.

As a coworker, boss, or business owner, we have many reasons to want to assist an abused employee. She might be somebody we have worked with side-by-side for many years. We might care deeply about this person's well being. We don't want anything bad to happen to her. We hate to see her face the pain of an abusive relationship. The bruises she disguises make us fear that worse will happen the next time supper is late or she forgets to take the garbage out.

As an employer, we have several reasons to be concerned. We care for the abused employee as a person and we detest seeing her in physical and/or emotional pain. We also have a significant amount of time and resources invested in the employee's training and education. A considerable amount of money has been invested to screen, hire, and place the employee. Replacing her with a new employee would be a costly proposition.

While the costs of replacing an employee depends on the skills needed to do the job, it is not uncommon for the cost projection of replacing an employee to be $10,000 or higher.

Managers are also concerned about the costs of the employee's decreased productivity. How can anybody give 110 percent to a job when his or her personal life is in a state of turmoil? It is unreasonable to take an employee who has not slept in days, is worried about feeding the children, or has bill collectors calling, and place her in the front office and expect her to be Mary Poppins.

Supervisors and managers should pay attention to the warning signs of domestic abuse. This may seem like meddling in an employee's personal life and it may feel very uncomfortable. Turn the situation around, and focus on the lost efficiency of the employee. View the situation as a managerial problem that must be resolved.

Abused employees frequently have evidence of bruises or broken bones. They may try to hide the bruises with makeup or wear long sleeved shirts and pants. They may say that they had an accident at home. Be suspicious when an employee professes to have experienced numerous accidents. People generally do not fall down the same set of stairs on a weekly basis, and they learn not to walk into walls after a couple of mishaps. Absenteeism and tardiness may increase due to the employee's doctor appointments. These situations seldom improve without intervention.

Abused employees may also suffer from depression, which could be evidenced by frequent crying or other observable symptoms. The employee might talk about suicide. Significant weight-gain or -loss might be readily observable.

As a supervisor or manager, you can be a resource for the abused employee. Remember, though, that you are neither a mental counselor nor a psychologist, and you should not pretend to be. Do not tell the employee what to do, and do not pretend to understand what she is going through. As a leader, you can help the employee in a variety of other ways.

Be empathetic to the employee's problems, and try to understand what the employee is going through and how she feels. Give the employee the opportunity to talk as much as she is willing to. Often, out of embarrassment or humiliation, abused employees are unwilling to give many details about the problems they face at home and the abuse they are facing. Listen to the employee talk; allow her to cry. You may be the only resource she has. Many times, abused women need somebody, anybody, to listen to them and show them support.

In many cases of marital abuse, the victim experiences a major lack of self-esteem. Allowing her to talk and offering empathy may make her feel much stronger than she felt before. In certain cases, the employee may feel a tremendous amount of relief by being able to expose the abuse to an empathetic ear.

Refer the victim to an employee assistance program (EAP) if one is available. If an EAP is not available, refer the employee to a community resource for battered spouses. Offer to stay in the room while the employee makes the initial call to either the EAP agency or the community resource. If the employee does not want you in the room, she will probably tell you so. If she does ask you to leave the room while she makes the initial call, tell her either that you will wait outside or that you will be back in ten or fifteen minutes. The circumstances will dictate the best route to take. Gentle prodding to pick up the telephone may be what the employee needs to start a recovery program. Do not try to force an employee to take actions that she doesn't want to take. You cannot make the status of an employee's personal life a condition of employment if the employee's job performance is otherwise acceptable. You can, however, make satisfactory performance of job-related duties a condition of employment.

Do not expect a miracle overnight just because the victim of domestic abuse does make the initial call. The employee is involved in a difficult situation, and there are no easy answers. It often takes years for the actual problem to develop, and it cannot be solved overnight. There are certain employees who will not be helped no matter what you do for them. Be prepared to face and accept this. After everything you do to help the employee, you must realize that the abused employee must take her own initiative in facing this problem and must make her own decisions. After all, she's the one who has to live with them.

In a worst-case scenario, the abuser may show up in the workplace. When this happens, the threat of violence enlarges to include all employees, customers, and visitors in the workplace. Most security professionals have dealt with this type of problem before.

In a typical situation, the abuser may show up at nine o'clock in the morning stone drunk. He has spent the last two or three hours in the local tavern, building his confidence and determining to set his wife straight. He shows up on the company doorstep with his own personal agenda and has no regard for security policy or procedure. The wife is usually highly embarrassed as her husband is escorted from the premise by security or law enforcement officers.

That situation is mild compared with other accounts we read in the daily papers. For example, on January 7, 1995, a forty-three-year-old man allegedly walked into the Ford Motor Plant in Plymouth Township, Michigan, with a gun. According to reports, he opened fire on his thirty-nine-year-old estranged wife, shooting her in the legs and the abdomen. Witnesses report that the man also shot a coworker, then turned the gun on himself. Both the wife and her coworker died shortly after the incident. This type of scenario is repeated all too often across the United States.

According to the U.S. Department of Labor, in 1992 a present or former spouse or boyfriend committed one-sixth of the incidents of violence against women in the workplace.[12] In a 2001 report released by the Department of Justice, the percentage of males victimizing females was 71 percent while the rate of females victimizing females was 25 percent.

In many incidents, the workplace is the only place where the assailant is sure to find the employee. A woman can change her address, her telephone number, even the car she drives—but it's less likely that she'll change employers. Her work habits stay the same and the estranged male usually knows what those work habits are.

STALKING

Even though stalking is a relatively new topic in the security field, it has existed for many years. Most experienced security professionals have been involved in an incident in which another person, often an employee's estranged spouse, stalked an employee.

In Schuyler, Nebraska, history repeated itself on March 3, 1995, when, for the second time since 1989, two employees were shot and killed in the parking lot of the Excel Corporation. In the latest incident, a man shot his common-law wife and the man with whom she had been living. Both victims died instantly after being shot in the head. The gunman then committed suicide. In November 1989, a man shot and killed his wife and her male companion in the same parking lot as they arrived for work. He was sentenced and convicted of the murders, and is now serving two consecutive life sentences.

Only recently have laws specifically related to stalking been passed. In 1990, California became the first state to pass anti-stalking legislation. Since then, almost all of the other states have followed suit and adopted similar legislation. The federal government has also enacted laws protecting women from violence. The Violence Against Women Act was passed in 1995 as part of the Crime Bill. The bill established the first Violence Against Women Office at the U.S. Department of Justice.

The language used in California's anti-stalking law was adopted by other states. In California, two major components are necessary for the stalking law to apply. First, a repeated pattern of harassment must be present. Following a person satisfies this component. The key word in the first component is *repeated*. Some states define *repeated* as simply more than once; other states have criteria that require two incidents within twenty-four hours. Second, an element of threat against the person must be present. Laws differ from state to state as to the level of threat required. In some states, the victim needs only to feel threatened; elsewhere, additional measures are required to determine the level of threat involved.

By September 1993, all states and the District of Columbia had adopted some form of anti-stalking laws. For more information on stalking laws applicable to your state, call your local law enforcement agency or go online to www.ncvc.org, the website of the National Center for Victims of Crime.

The workplace is the prime target for stalkers to pursue their victims. Like victims of domestic abuse, stalking victims can change their home telephone number, the vehicle they drive, and even move to a new house or apartment. One thing they usually cannot easily change is jobs. The victims still go to places of business on the same days at the same time. Chances are they sit at the same desk, have the same lunch and break schedule, and park in the same areas. Stalkers, especially estranged spouses, know the habits of their victims.

Victims of stalkers may find notes on their cars, receive unwanted flowers, numerous telephone calls, and suffer a host of other nuisances. Stalkers usually follow their victims constantly and know where they are at all times.

Victims are often not willing to let company security officials know that they are being stalked until the situation becomes dangerous. They may be reluctant to talk to a stranger about such a personal subject. Victims of stalking may live in quiet desperation, not knowing where to turn and not wanting others to know their fears and anxieties. In some circumstances, they may not call the police for fear of enraging the stalker. When the victim is fearful of the potential actions of the stalker, police assistance can be little help. When the victim does call the police, they may be unable to help because a crime has not yet been committed. When the police do get involved, it may end up as one person's word against the other's. This is especially true when the two parties have had a previous intimate relationship. Some states have specific laws regarding these types of cases.

Cases of stalking have continued for years. One woman stalked David Letterman for six years. She had posed as his wife and broken into his house numerous times. Once, when Letterman was out of town, she stole his car and drove it for several days before being caught. Injunctions did little to resolve the matter. Between 1988 and 1993, the woman was arrested eight times. Her eventual death put an end to one of the most publicized celebrity stalking cases ever.

Rebecca Schaeffer, the star of "My Sister Sam" was the stalking victim of an obsessed fan. It all ended tragically on July 1989, when she opened her apartment door and was fatally shot in the chest with a .357 magnum. The stalker was arrested and convicted of murder. He is now in prison, serving a life sentence without the possibility of parole. The tragedy touched the hearts of the nation, as people became painfully aware of the case through heartfelt statements by Rebecca Schaeffer's family, friends, and coworkers. Costar Pam Dawber faced the cameras and shared her anguish as she mourned the loss of her friend and coworker.

Celebrity stalking cases can get a great deal of media attention, but the symptoms of a pursued employee in the company may not be so evident. The employer can be made aware of the stalking in a number of ways. Ideally, the stalking victims should go to the security department for assistance, but this does not always happen. A friend or coworker may talk to security officers about the situation out of fear for the victim's safety or their own. The supervisor or manager may become aware of the situation after observing a decrease in productivity or performance. Security officers may discover the truth after incidents in the parking lot. The receptionist may suspect the problem when the employee repeatedly refuses telephone calls, flowers, or other deliveries from a particular individual. Once, I observed a female employee receive thirteen dozen roses in a single day from an estranged boyfriend trying to make amends. Each delivery came from a different florist and was purchased on a stolen credit card. By the end of the day, the employee was a nervous wreck, the security department was involved, and the paperwork for an injunction was filed.

The security or human resources department may become aware that a problem exists after other employees report suspicious activities involving the stalker or the victim. Employees who report this type of problem should be allowed to remain anonymous.

Another type of stalking case involves employees (current or former) who stalk supervisory or managerial personnel. The supervisor who fires or disciplines an employee may become the center of the employee's frustrations. The employee may feel that the action taken by management was personally motivated and may, as a result, begin a campaign to destroy the supervisor's life. The crusade may include such typical stalking actions as repeated threats, phone calls, e-mails, following the victim, or sitting outside the person's home or office.

Romantic obsession, or erotomania, takes place when one person is the recipient of the unwanted affections of another person. The stalker develops an obsession with the victim and believes that fate has bound them together. The employee on the receiving end of this obsession often experiences an overwhelming display of the other person's fixation. If the stalking victim is involved with another person, that person is often the target of death threats. Because this other person stands in the way of the stalker's desire to become involved with the victim, the stalker believes that by taking the third party out of the picture, he or she will succeed in winning the victim's affection.

Once the company becomes aware that a problem exists, it faces a dilemma: What actions should be taken to protect not only the targeted employee, but all employees? Businesses generally frown on getting involved in their employees' personal problems, even when just cause for concern exists. Simply referring the employee to an EAP offers very little protection for the company or the employee. A more aggressive action plan is often advisable in a stalking situation. Emotional support is beneficial, but not a cure-all for the employee in the situation. Larger cities may have support groups for victims. A support group may provide emotional support to the employee as well as offer practical advice on ways for victims to protect themselves. The other members of the support group may have encountered, or still encounter, the same feelings and experiences. (See the box "Tips for Victims of Stalking.")

Tips for Victims of Stalking

1. Document every contact with the stalker. This includes all telephone calls, messages, letters, deliveries, and all cases of being followed or watched. This documentation will help you prove that you are being stalked.

2. Contact the police department every time the stalker makes any kind of contact. The police department should also maintain documentation. Obtain copies of all police reports and incident numbers.

3. Use an answering machine or caller-identification service to screen calls. Have a trace put on your phone to record the times the stalker calls and change to an unlisted phone number. Give the new phone number only to people who need to know. Consider using a pager to screen emergency calls. A cell phone can provide access to emergency services when you are in your car or away from the telephone. Many police and sheriff offices provide free cell phones tied directly to 911 to stalking victims.

4. Advise your friends, neighbors, coworkers, and family members of the situation. Have neighbors watch for any unusual activity at or near your home.

5. Keep the outside of your home well lit and free of excessive bushes or trees that might provide a stalker a place to hide.

6. Install extra locks, lights, and door alarms. If you can afford it, use a security monitoring service. Consider getting a large dog.

7. Join a support group or seek other outside support. Get assistance from local agencies.

8. File an injunction against the stalker. Keep a copy of the injunction with you at all times. Talk to an attorney about other legal tactics.

9. Never enter into any conversation with the stalker. Most stalkers are very persuasive and are able to solicit a response (typically an angry one) from the victim.

10. Consider enrolling in a self-defense class. Pepper spray and mace are good self-defense tools if you know how to use them properly.

> Don't automatically buy a gun. Weapons can be dangerous to have around and can lead to other problems. If you do have a gun, make sure you know how to use it proficiently.
>
> 11. Keep another person around you as much as possible when running errands.

In many ways, the profile of the stalker mirrors that of the potentially violent person (discussed in the next chapter). Although the majority of cases involve men stalking women, women also stalk men, such as in the case of David Letterman.

REFERENCES

1. Bureau of Justice Statistics, Special Report. *Violence in the Workplace 1993-99.*(Washington D.C.: U.S. Government Printing Office, December 2001), page 1.

2. "SHRM Reveals Extent of Workplace Violence," *EAP Digest* (March-April 1994) 25

3. Bureau of Justice Statistics, Special Report. *Violence in the Workplace 1993-99.*(Washington D.C.: U.S. Government Printing Office, December 2001), page 1.

4. Alcohol, Drug Abuse, and Mental Health Administration, U.S. Department of Health and Human Services, *The Economic Costs of Alcohol and Drug Abuse and Mental Illness: 1985* (Washington, D.C.: U.S. Government Printing Office, 1990).

5. L.D. Johnson, P.M. O'Malley, and J.G. Bachman, *National Survey Results on Drug Use from the Monitoring the Future Survey, 1975-1993* (Washington, D.C.: U.S. Department of Health and Human Services, 1994), pp. 6-9.

6. "Why the Violence? Workers Respond," *EAP Digest* (March-April 1994): 10.

7. F.J. Dickman, W.G. Emener, and W.S. Hutchinson, Jr., *Counseling the Troubled Person in Industry* (Springfield, IL: Thomas Publications, 1985), p. 23.

8. Lisa Genasci, "More Companies See Domestic Violence as a Workplace Issue," *Waterloo Courier*, 25 December 1994, p. B1.

9. U.S. Department of Labor, Bureau of Labor Statistics, *News*, 10 August 1994, p. 3.

10. S. Glazer, "Violence Against Women," *CQ Researcher* 3 (February 1993): 171.

11. *Statistics Package*, 3rd ed. (Philadelphia: National Clearinghouse for the Defense of Battered Women, February 1994), p. 91.

12. J. Windau and G. Toscano, *Workplace Homicides in 1992* (Washington, D.C.: U.S. Department of Labor, Bureau of Labor Statistics, February 1994), p. 2.

PROFILES OF THE VIOLENT PERSON

Establishing profiles of the disgruntled employee who may return to work in a violent manner is a dangerous proposition. Stereotyping employees into narrowly defined classifications could establish a propensity to look for employees who fit the profiles and ignore threats or intimidations made by others. There is not one certain genetic makeup of the violent employee. Employee violence is committed by a spectrum of people under a variety of circumstances.

However, based on the case histories of workplace violence, researchers have developed a profile into which a significant portion of the offenders fit. Most offenders are white males between the ages of twenty-five and forty-five. They have been employed with the same employer for a long period of time (that is, they are typically not a new or a temporary employee), and they often have strong personal ties with their job.

The profile has limited value to the employer. Profiles do not serve as an indicator of future violence. They only serve to describe workers who have in the past returned violently to the workplace. Behaviors and warning should be used to evaluate the level of danger that might exist. When determining the mental condition of an employee, the first thing you must look at is the individual's behavior. As with counseling and coaching, the focus of an employee profiling must be the behavior of the employee and not his or her physical characteristics. The employee's behavior is the key to intervention and prevention of violence. (See the box "Assessing the Violent Person.")

Assessing the Violent Person

1. Do not depend on profiles to predict violent behavior.

2. There is no all-inclusive list of predictable behaviors for violent individuals.

3. Model employees have behaved violently.

---

4. You must evaluate an employee's behavior to determine his or her propensity for violence.

5. People who are known to have a history of violence may have a tendency for violence in the future.

6. Claims of the exotic or strange may indicate that an employee is losing touch with reality.

7. Alcohol and drug abuse are common among people who have committed violence in the workplace.

8. After incidents of workplace violence, many people say the disgruntled employee had a fascination with weapons or other incidents of workplace violence.

9. Employees who say, "What happened there could happen here," may be issuing a warning of their own future actions.

10. Employees who directly threaten the use of violence probably really do mean it.

WARNING SIGNS OF VIOLENT BEHAVIOR

You can help protect your company from acts of aggression by learning to identify the signs that precede violence by employees, customers, or visitors and by following the recommended guidelines. Once you've learned to recognize these signs, you must respond in an appropriate manner to the perceived level of the threat. If the warning signs indicate an immediate danger, immediately notify the local police or sheriff's department. If the indications point to future acts of aggression, alert the company's human resources and security departments. The intervention plan must meet the degree of the threat anticipated.

There is no single all-inclusive list of predictable behaviors that a violent person will exhibit. There are, however, common indicators that mark a person's disposition to engage in violent acts. (See the box "Warning Signs of Violent Behavior.") Caution must be exercised in interpreting these warning signs. One warning sign, if significant, may be all that's needed to determine that additional evaluation is required. However, victims of violent acts by a coworker usually agree that more than one warning sign was present.

Warning Signs of Violent Behavior

- Threats of physical violence or statements about getting even

- History of violence against coworkers, family members, other people, or animals

- History of failed relationships with family members, spouses, friends, coworkers

- Lack of social support system (i.e., friends and family)

- Paranoia and distrust of others

- Stating that certain people are out to get him/her

- Blaming others for life's failures and problems

- Claims of strange events, such as visits from UFO's

- Alcohol or drug abuse on or off the job

- Frequent tardiness and absenteeism

- Concentration, performance, or safety-related problems

- Carrying or concealing a weapon at work (security officers, police officers, etc. excepted)

- Obsession with weapons, often exotic weapons

- Fascination with stories of violence, especially those that happened at the workplace, such as frequent discussions of post office slayings

- History of intimidation against other people

- High levels of frustration, easily angered

- Diminished self-esteem

- No personal responsibility

- Inability to handle stressful situations

- Romantic obsession with a coworker

In at least one situation, this was not the case. John Taylor had always been considered a model employee at the Orange Glen Post Office in California. Taylor had received numerous awards for his good job performance. He was well liked and enjoyed social relationships with friends and coworkers. Underneath his model behavior, however, something must have been very wrong. On August 10, 1989, Taylor shot and killed his wife in their home before he went to work. He brought one hundred rounds of ammunition and a .22 caliber semiautomatic weapon with him that day. He killed two coworkers and injured another before killing himself. Even after the rampage, most coworkers felt that he had always been an exemplary employee. The employees were left struggling to determine what could have gone so wrong in Taylor's life that he felt that this was his only solution. A suicide note found at his residence indicated he had been hurting a lot and only had pain to look forward to. He did not have a known history of alcohol or drug abuse and he had no criminal history.

In the case of multiple homicides that took place at the University of Arizona in October 2002, the shooter, 41-year-old student Robert Steward Flores, Jr., displayed many of the warning signs of violence. According to other students, Mr. Flores often exhibited aggressive and angry behavior. Mr. Flores allegedly bragged to other students about receiving a concealed weapons permit and had threatened to blow up the building.

THREATS

Employees who make comments about getting even with managers, supervisors, or other employees for disciplinary actions or dismissals should be taken very seriously. The follow-up to these threats can range from flattening tires to murder. The degree of the threat depends on what is said and the manner in which it is said.

Almost everybody in the security and human resources professions has heard a seemingly simple comment that made the hair on the back of their neck stand on end. Without the need for additional words, the insinuation was clear. The manner of what is said and the appropriateness of the remark are clues to possible future actions. When in doubt report the conversation to others whom can assist you—perhaps the human resources or security departments. If you are a member of either of these departments, don't hesitate to make the conversation known to others on your team. The threats may be idle, or they may not. Until the intent is known, caution must be exercised.

Ignored threats can lead to tragedy. In Royal Oaks, Michigan, thirty-one-year-old postal worker Thomas McIlvane told many people his intentions to kill many of his coworkers. He also made threats by telephone. He had a history of extensive violence and had been reprimanded on several occasions. On November 14, 1991, McIlvane followed through on his threats. Before turning the gun on himself, he engaged in a shooting rampage that left four of his coworkers dead and four others wounded. McIlvane died two days later from his self-inflicted injuries. Part of his violent past included driving an M-60 tank over an automobile while in the Marine Corps.

HISTORY OF VIOLENCE

People who are known to have committed acts of violence against family members, fellow employees, acquaintances, or animals should be considered as having a propensity towards violence. They have already exhibited behaviors that show a lack of respect for others. This is one of the reasons why background checks on applicants for employment are vital to the well being of any business. People typically act as they have acted before, and history has a way of repeating itself. If a potential employee has a history of assaults or threats, the company may be best suited in the long run to keep looking for other candidates. (More is covered on this topic in Chapter 6.)

HISTORY OF FAILED RELATIONSHIPS

Employees known to have a history of failed relationships with spouses, family members, or friends may lack the support network that many people take for granted. Employees who have no other resources available for venting their concerns or frustrations to somebody who has a genuine concern for their well being may be a potential problem. Imagine for a moment a frustrated employee who is very upset with management for whatever reason and has nobody to vent to. The frustration can build and build to the point of an explosive response. Employee-assistance programs can provide some support for these people and should not be overlooked as a resource. Employees who commit violence in the workplace often do not have family or friends in whom they feel they can confide.

Potentially violent employees may also have a history of interpersonal conflicts with coworkers, especially supervisory and management personnel. They may be unable to maintain good relationships with others for any period of time, or they may abandon relationships with other employees or family members. They may also isolate themselves from society. They often sit alone on breaks and during lunch due to their inability to develop and maintain relationships with coworkers.

DISTRUST AND SUSPICION

An employee's failure to get along with others, especially supervisors and managers, can lead to distrust and suspicion. Potentially violent employees may have a severe distrust of others. They may blame others for their problems and refuse to accept any level of personal responsibility. They may believe that everybody is out to get them. Increased errors might be blamed on other employees purposely sabotaging their work. They may claim that the manager or supervisor is planning on terminating their employment for a variety of reasons. In many of these situations, the employer may not be contemplating any action against the employee. The employee creates the delusions as a result of his or her paranoia.

When the supervisor does try to counsel potentially violent employees to improve their job performance or behavior, the employee may refuse to accept any type of coaching and take all statements as personal criticism. Long-lasting grudges may develop. To employees like this, the supervisor or manager may become the nucleus of their perceived injustice and all of their personal and professional problems. This nucleus can expand to include human resources, union representatives, or others whom the employee feels is part of the conspiracy. Many employees who return to the workplace to kill their coworkers are target driven. Their supervisors, managers, human resources professionals, or union representatives are often on the list of victims.

This was the case when Paul Hannah, a lineman for the telephone company in Chicago, was suspended for refusing to take a drug test. He shot at the company manager, but the gun misfired six times. The gun eventually fired properly, and the union steward who tried to intervene was killed.

In times when layoffs are pending and everybody in the company feels a lack of job security, emotionally distressed employees will have exaggerated feelings of paranoia and distrust. Because they are often on the targeted layoff list due to already poor performance, they may sabotage other employees' work to make their own performance look better. When they do receive their pink slip or demotion due to downsizing, they feel their suspicions were proven, regardless of the underlying reasons. They may say things like, "I told you so but nobody would listen." If the company's management does not recognize the threat, the unstable employee could go unnoticed until he or she shows up at the receptionist's desk one day with a gun. This obviously means that too little attention was given to the threat, too late. There are no winners.

This was the case in Tampa, Florida, in 1992, when Paul Calden returned to his former workplace, Fireman's Insurance Company. When he had been fired eight months earlier, he told employees "You ain't seen the last of me." When Calden returned, he shot the human resources manager, saying, "This is what you get for firing me." In total, three men died and two women were injured. Calden later killed himself.

UNUSUAL CLAIMS

Claims of the exotic and strange could be an indication that an employee is losing contact with reality and suffering from mental illness. When employees claim to have had personal visits from aliens, the President of the United States, Napoleon, or Jesus Christ, there is real reason for concern. Referral to an employee-assistance program or an intervention plan should be implemented immediately.

ALCOHOL OR DRUG ABUSE

Alcohol or drug abuse is a common malady of people who commit acts of violence in the workplace as current or former employees, customers, or others. Alcohol and drugs can lower inhibitions and grant a false sense of security.

Money is often the motivation for criminal act in cases such as robbery. The offender needs money to support a habit, and other means of obtaining money may not be available.

Employees facing drug or alcohol problems can be referred to an employee-assistance program for help. When job-related performance problems like absenteeism and tardiness are a result of substance abuse, the employee should be referred. As a supervisor, you cannot make an employee accept help for an addiction, but you can make it known that future employment depends on improved job performance.

OWNERSHIP OF WEAPONS

Employees who are known to own weapons or belong to clubs in which weapons are the major focus could be considered capable of procuring weapons that might later be used against other employees. However, caution needs to be exercised in profiling gun owners as violent or dangerous people. In the majority of cases, owning a gun in the United States is legal. In the United States, bearing arms is a constitutional right—a right that many citizens actively exercise. Major organizations, such as the National Rifle Association (NRA), provide lobbying support in the crusade to retain the right to own and carry weapons. Millions of Americans own guns for self-protection, hunting, sportsmanship, investments, or other personal reasons. Most people who legally own weapons do not do so to commit criminal acts against others. Ownership of weapons is a personal choice for almost everybody, except minors, convicted felons, and people convicted of domestic abuse. Much like abortion, gambling, and religion, the right to bear arms is a topic that reeks of political, emotional, and moral dilemmas.

Mandatory waiting periods for weapon-purchase permits are typically referred to as *cooling-off-periods*. People who want to purchase a weapon as a means to express an irrational and often violent action will have the opportunity and the time to calm themselves down and take care of whatever problems they may be trying to resolve in a more productive manner. The cooling-off period also allows the issuing agency time to investigate the applicant's background for prior criminal convictions and/or a history of mental instability.

Employees who keep loaded weapons at home or in their vehicles have almost immediate access to them, and hence the calming down period is not available. Never assume that an employee has a license to carry a gun. Even when the employee does display a license, the employer can still ban weapons from company-owned property. Weapons are not appropriate in the work environment. Employees who threaten to use weapons against others are an immediate concern, whether they have a weapon in their possession or not.

Anytime you discover that an employee has carried a weapon into the workplace, you must take immediate action. Notify local police to assist in the intervention. Managers, supervisors, and human resource people should not confront an armed employee alone. You may be asked to assist the police department in determining the level of immediate danger present.

It could be that an employee with a shotgun in his truck forgot to put it away when he returned from a hunting trip. In this situation, the employee will most likely understand that intervention is necessary to ensure the safety and security of the other employees. On the other hand, an employee with a history of threats of intimidation may not appreciate the police showing up to remove the weapon—but at that point, who cares? Threats in the workplace create a climate of fear that can affect employees as dramatically as actual violence. Employees who are afraid may not show up for work, and those who do will not be productive.[1]

Your company has a legal obligation to provide a safe and secure work environment free from all recognized hazards. Obviously, a disgruntled employee with a weapon is a big hazard, and you must exercise extreme caution. Employee safety is the primary concern; protecting the company from civil lawsuits is secondary.

FASCINATION WITH WEAPONS

Disgruntled employees who have committed violence against coworkers often owned or talked about highly exotic weapons. This fascination frequently includes a passion for weapons that are not typically associated with self-defense, hunting, or common gun collecting. Potentially violent employees may own a large number of exotic weapons, such as automatic rifles with elaborate scopes, AK47s, swords, knifes, bayonets, and the like.

The exotic weapons fixation turned deadly in Irvine, California, on June 30, 2003, when former employee Joseph Hunter Parker returned to his former workplace with a samurai-style sword. Joseph Hunter Parker had left his job bagging groceries in a grocery store. Media accounts state that Parker collected swords and was a fan of the movie "Highlander." Parker was a diagnosed schizophrenic and described as a loner. Parker was killed by police in the incident. He was 30 years old.

FASCINATION WITH WORKPLACE VIOLENCE

Another indication that an employee may use violence or intimidation to rectify a perceived injustice, or in some cases a real injustice, is a fixation on incidents of workplace violence. The employee may frequently talk about post office slayings or other cases where a worker used violence.

It is common for employees to discuss incidents of violence that have occurred in their city or at an affiliated business. Some of this talk is productive, as it enables employees to discuss their feelings with others in a supportive environment. After acts of workplace violence, it can be therapeutic and aid in the healing process when employees share their feelings with coworkers.

However, employees who say things like, "What happened there could happen here," may be issuing a warning of their own actions. When this type of statement is made in conjunction with other warning signs, a serious situation is developing and an intervention plan should be implemented.

HISTORY OF HARASSMENT OR INTIMIDATION

When employees harass and intimidate their coworkers, you must deal with them in a swift and impartial fashion. A no-tolerance corporate policy must be enforced for the benefit of all employees.

When you fail to deal with intimidation, you send a signal that the company condones this type of behavior. Productivity will suffer, and the organization could lose valuable long-term employees who choose to work in a less hostile work environment.

In summary, employees who do not fit the typical mold, feel they are being persecuted by others, have little or no support from friends and family, talk excessively about exotic events (including politics, religion, and visits from unlikely people), and are known to have ready access to firearms may be your biggest threat. Take them seriously. To ignore an employee who is threatening and intimidating people at work is to encourage more of the same.[2]

REFERENCES

1. B. Filipczak, "Armed and Dangerous at Work," *Training* (July 1993): 41

2. Ibid., 41.

PART TWO
BEFORE WORKPLACE VIOLENCE OCCURS

CHAPTER FOUR

INGREDIENTS FOR A VOLATILE WORKPLACE

Violence that erupts in the workplace is like a recipe. When the wrong ingredients are mixed together, a very dangerous, yet predictable, outcome can occur. (See the box "Ingredients for a Volatile Workplace.")

Many managerial books were written during the last twenty-five years. Each one of these claims the "right" way to conduct the business of employing people. Few of these books on the various styles and philosophies of managerial behavior appear today on the MBA reading lists. As times are changing, a new, more humane and responsive management style is emerging. The autocratic management style, in which the supervisor figuratively stands over the employee with a whip, is no longer acceptable. Productivity and employee satisfaction improve when the workplace is an environment of trust and respect. People want to be treated with respect and consideration. When managers and supervisors forget this key element, they create an environment that is ripe for trouble. The experts who have studied workplace killings nearly all agree that many times a contributing factor was a rigid, almost paramilitary work culture.[1]

Ingredients for a Volatile Workplace

- The highly competitive nature of business causes high levels of stress for employees, supervisors, and managers.

- Problems between labor and management can create an "us vs. them" atmosphere among some employees.

- Work environments that produce a large number of grievances can be conducive to acts of workplace violence.

- Certain kinds of stress are productive, but a high level of stress can be very destructive and can later foster an environment conducive to violence.

- Rigid, almost paramilitary work cultures foster bitterness and resentment that can produce violent behavior.

Ideally, every employee will accept the company's mission statement and adopt its goals on a personal level. The truth is that many employees either never adopt the company philosophy or stop believing in it. They see themselves as there to collect a paycheck and sometimes do a job. They could not care less about return on equity, strategic business plans, and the like as long as these things don't affect their job security. These employees have a personal agenda; they are just trying to earn a living before going home at the end of the day. They don't want extra hours or extra responsibilities unless the pay makes it worthwhile. This is neither entirely right nor wrong; it's just the way things are.

When these employees exist in a company—and all companies have them—management may try to force them into different departments or try to encourage higher levels of productivity from them. How many of us have seen supervisors elevate an employee's performance report when a problem employee applies for a different job in a different department? It seems like pawning problem employees off on someone else is a common solution when dealing with them. Global competition is forcing every company to get the most out of every resource, including employees. When the competitor's employees are more dedicated and productive than yours, the future of your company may be at stake. Management is under tremendous pressure to produce results.

When management makes changes that demand more from employees, some of the employees will resent these actions. Problems can easily develop between labor and management. Labor-management disputes are characteristic of work environments that are conducive to employee violence. An upset employee may feel wrongfully charged with acts of workplace misconduct or poor performance. Remember that one of the characteristics of potentially dangerous employees is paranoia—in this case, the belief that management is out to get them. Management that responds poorly to the needs of employees can perpetuate these feelings in a dysfunctional person.

Work environments that produce a multitude of grievances by employees are also indicative of trouble. Management must take a serious look at the types of grievances filed by employees to determine the problems that exist. If the grievances lead to the realization that employees are unhappy with the company's management style, the company needs to take this matter to heart.

What changes can be made to improve employee attitudes? Are the grievances centered around a specific person or department? Are the complaints symptomatic of deep-rooted problems within the company? For now, don't even consider the propensity for violence; just think about the damage to your company's bottom line. Unhappy employees are less productive, and your company risks losing valued employees to other, less distressed businesses. Employees are the greatest and most valuable assets that your company has. Just as a construction company doesn't leave its wood out to rot, don't leave your employees rotting in bitterness and resentment.

The anger and rage of unhappy employees can be expressed in the form of increased work-related accidents. Workers who are upset and preoccupied with labor problems pay less attention to their jobs. They may feel rushed, or simply may not care about the job they're doing. They may not pay attention to what is going on around them because they are focused on the latest rumors and gossip.

An increase in the number of on-the-job accidents means an increase in the number of worker compensation claims. Employees who believe that the company owes them more than what they are getting may use an accident claim to get what they want; a large settlement, an extended "paid vacation" to recover from their alleged injuries, or attention from their peers. Whatever the cause of on-the-job accidents or the motivations of an employee filing a claim, the increased costs and lost productivity are not in the best interests of the company.

Claims of stress-related disabilities are gaining widespread popularity. In the vast majority of cases, the attending physician or psychiatrist finds the employer responsible for a significant portion of the stress. During an interview, Kenneth Wernimont, a clinical social worker, noted that as many as 30 percent of the patients who seek professional counseling do so as the result of job-induced stresses. In these cases, the company must actively work with the employee and his or her doctor, mental-health provider, and the workers' compensation insurance carrier.

When the employee's claim is perfectly valid, you will want to start re-solving the problems and get the employee back to work at least part-time. When the claim is less than legitimate, be prepared for the big ride. Stress claims can result in huge disability settlements and enormous paid leaves of absence. Add the presence of many attorneys willing to help convince your employees of their illnesses and you're looking at a fight your company would rather avoid. Preventing stress claims is less expensive than resolving them later.

There is no denying that stress exists in nearly every workplace in the United States and abroad. Certain levels of stress are needed to promote a productive and satisfying work environment. Most people operate more efficiently when they are faced with a moderate amount of stress. How each person handles stress is important.

Think of the report due in the near future. You will probably keep the deadline for the report in mind as you schedule your other work-related activities. Ideally, you will have time to complete the report in a satisfactory manner and turn it in. Knowing that the report is due keeps you working towards accomplishing that goal. What would happen if the deadline for the report was set back a year? Most people would drop it off their to-do list in a heartbeat and move on to other more pressing things. Without a new deadline, the report may never get done. The stress created by deadlines keeps people focused on getting the job done. Remove the deadline, hence the stress, and the motivation for completing job assignments diminishes and productivity goes down.

Another example of productive stress occurs almost daily in a company in my hometown. Chances are this is repeated, in some form, at other businesses across the globe. The business rewards employees for consistently exceeding annual profit goals. When the company exceeds profit goals by a predetermined percentage, the company treats all of the employees and their spouses to either a Caribbean cruise or an exotic vacation in Mexico.

The employees win the company-sponsored trip almost every time it's offered. They work together and do what it takes to succeed. This can mean long hours and overtime on weekends. Scrap materials and defects in quality are kept to a minimum. Peer pressure exists to keep all employees working as productively as possible. Employees who work for this company are proud of their jobs and proud to be associated with the company. The stress to exceed annual profit goals and win the trip works out to everybody's advantage. This type of atmosphere creates a win-win situation. Management is happy, the stockholders are happy, and the employees are happy.

Certainly not all companies can offer cruises and vacations to all employees. The gist of it is that the company promotes a healthy work environment and productivity is maximized. This principle can be applied to all businesses. Make your employees happy, and they will repay your efforts. Build an atmosphere of distrust and dispute, and your employees will also repay those efforts—nobody wins.

CORPORATE POLICIES AND PROCEDURES

Reducing violence in the workplace starts at the top of the corporate ladder, but it must involve everyone. Every employee in the workplace, from the chief executive officer to the night janitor, has a responsibility to him- or herself, to the company, and to the community to reduce violence in the workplace. Just as it takes all of the members of the work group to produce a piece of equipment, the entire team of employees must make a solid commitment to ensure a safe and secure working environment. Although each employee will have a different role to play, all roles are increasingly important.

Starting with the chief executive officer, president, team leader, or whoever leads the way in managing the company, a commitment must be made to provide protection for all employees from intimidation, harassment, threats, and violence. Without this commitment, all other efforts will surely fail due to lack of managerial support. Managerial support must be strong and unquestionable. This commitment does not necessarily mean that the managerial staff will become involved in investigating each case of possible harassment. It does mean that management will support the staff that is charged with conducting the investigation. A written public statement shows support for those who must decide how to deal with employees who violate the norms of expected social behavior.

Give every employee in the company, including all new hires, a copy of the company policy regarding workplace harassment, intimidation, and threats. Translate the policy into whatever languages your employees speak. Require each employee to read and sign the statement, and keep a copy of the signed statement in the employee's personnel file. Later, if the employee is found to have violated this policy, you will be better able to justify discipline, up to and including termination. (See the box "Corporate Policies and Procedures.")

Corporate Policies and Procedures

- Top management is responsible for reducing workplace violence.

- A written policy prohibiting violence, harassment, and threats must be clearly posted and communicated to all employees.

- Policies and procedures relative to workplace violence must be written, taught, and followed.

- All employees have a responsibility to assist in providing a safe and healthful work environment free of all known hazards.

- All employees who are found to have violated this policy should face disciplinary action, up to and including termination.

To assist you in establishing your own written statement on workplace violence, a sample policy is provided. (See the box "Sample Policy Statement on Workplace Violence.")

The statement can, and should, be modified to meet the unique needs of your organization.

Sample Policy Statement on Workplace Violence

It is the policy of [Name of Business] to provide a safe and secure work environment for all employees. We aim to provide a work atmosphere that promotes trust, fairness, and achievement for employees. [Name of Business] expressly prohibits all acts of intimidation, harassment, and threatening behavior.

Employees have a responsibility to themselves, other employees, and the company to report all incidents of intimidation and harassment, as well as other safety and security related matters occurring in the workplace. All reports will be thoroughly investigated by management staff. Any employee found to be in violation of this policy will be subject to disciplinary action, including possible termination.

LEGAL ASPECTS OF A SECURE WORK ENVIRONMENT

Furnishing a safe and secure work environment is not only the right thing to do; it's also a legal responsibility. Failing to provide a secure work environment could lead to civil or criminal liabilities. The legal repercussions could affect both the company and the people responsible for providing a safe work environment.

After any death in the workplace, regardless of the reasons for the death, among the first people to show up at the work site will be officials from the Occupational Safety and Health Administration (OSHA). If the death was a result of the employer's failure to provide a safe and healthful work environment, the company could face severe fines. The personnel responsible for providing a safe and secure work environment could also be held personally liable for the death. If OSHA finds an individual personally responsible for a workplace death or injury, he or she could face both criminal and civil prosecution. Although rare, jail time and personal fines could result.

In a landmark case, OSHA cited Charter Barkley Hospital in Chicago for failing to provide a safe work environment under OSHA's General Duty Clause, Section 5 (a)(1). The citation was issued in September of 1993 for not having safeguards in place to protect workers from violent patients. Since the citation, the hospital has initiated training programs and other measures to prevent violence in the hospital.

Other potential problems could arise under worker's compensation cases when employees are injured or killed while performing their duties. Employees and survivors can file a claim against the company not only for their injury, but also for lost wages, stress disabilities, and permanent losses as a result of death or injury.

Some businesses believe that they cannot afford to provide safety-related training and security equipment. However, compare the cost of the training and equipment to that of paying for surgery for a gunshot wound. The surgery and the hospital stay could easily cost $100,000, and this doesn't include the cost of lost wages and permanent disabilities. The final amount will be even higher if an employee or customer dies as a result of an attack.

Negligent hiring lawsuits could surface from employees and the their families if a company is found to have not fulfilled its legal responsibilities regarding preemployment screening. Courts have already established that a company has a duty to protect employees and customers from other workers that the company knows, or should have known, posed a risk to others. Employers should conduct preemployment screening to weed out potential problems.

Allowing a hostile work environment to exist also creates a legal issue for employers. The failure to provide proper supervision has resulted in lawsuits.

REFERENCE

1. H.F. Bensimon, "Violence in the Workplace," *Training and Development Journal* (January 1994): 27.

EMPLOYEE EDUCATION

The responsibility for security must rest with all employees. From a security standpoint, the employees are the eyes and the ears of the business. They are privy to the conversations taking place in the break rooms, locker rooms, and washrooms. They are the ones who hear the threats, stories, and rumors before managers, supervisors, and security professionals do. When an employee identifies and reports a potential security problem, the problem can be investigated and resolved before it escalates, and losses can be mitigated. Security managers should not overlook employees as a resource for information. Try to tap this resource. Actively solicit the support and cooperation of your employees in preventing workplace violence.

Everybody's overall safety program must include employee training. Employers can expect to be hit with a lawsuit if they fail to provide safety and security related training and an employee is injured or killed during an incident of workplace violence. As stated earlier, the courts have ruled that employers are responsible for providing employees with a safe and secure work environment.

Employees need to be educated on a variety of security and safety related topics. Training for all employees should include general security awareness, personal responsibility to ensure security, and recognizing and responding to aggressive behavior from coworkers, customers, and others at the workplace. Employees who work with money and other valuables must be taught how to act during and immediately following a robbery. Robbery deterrence should also be taught. The location and operation of alarms should be covered for employees who work in the vicinity of panic alarms. Employees who may be called to assist in apprehending a shoplifter must know how to do this in a safe and legal manner. Robbery training is covered in Chapter 8.

Educating employees about the signs of potentially aggressive or violent behavior can diminish the likelihood of violence striking your business. Employees need to know what to report and to whom. Employees at all levels of the organization should be taught how to recognize potentially destructive behavior *and* how to respond to it. The response should include reporting procedures in both emergency and non-emergency circumstances. Identification is of little use without evaluation and intervention.

Most employers want to do the right thing when it comes to helping maintain a safe facility, but without the proper training they might react poorly to volatile situations because they do not know what is expected of them. For example, consider an office worker who sees an unauthorized, unfamiliar person wandering around a restricted area. If the employee does not know what is expected of her, she must decide how to respond to the trespasser. Her possible decisions include the following:

- Ignore the situation.

- Confront the intruder immediately.

- Find another employee and then confront the intruder.

- Contact a supervisor or manager.

- Contact building security.

- Contact local law enforcement.

The expected employee response should have already been defined during training. What if the intruder is a young woman with a child looking for a restroom? In many instances calling the police would be an overreaction. However, what if the intruder is a 6'10" man weighing 275 pounds? If employees feel uncomfortable or intimidated by the prospect of confronting a stranger, it is probably best that they don't. Unless you provide employees with guidance on whom to call, you leave them in a no-win situation. The decision to act or not to act also depends on the business environment and the associated risks (nuclear plant vs. grocery store).

Companies that lack the resources to employ an in-house security or training professional can contract with consultants to conduct the training. Safety and security training should be conducted for all new employees and should be reviewed at least annually, or when a change in job duties occurs. Training review is also very beneficial after any significant incidents or threats. Employees should be allowed to provide input into the curriculum since they often have specific concerns. Ample time should be allowed for questions at the end of the program. Instructors should also inform employees that they are available to discuss concerns privately.

In some instances, state laws dictate the extent and frequency of employee security and safety training. Check with legal counsel about the laws in your area. Consider state-mandated training to be the minimum requirement. Give employees as much training as they need to carry out their job responsibilities in a safe manner. With the recent increased awareness of violence in the workplace, terrorism, and the growing number of regulations that businesses must comply with, it's only a matter of time before all businesses will be required by law to provide security training. (See the box "Training Topics.")

MANAGER AND SUPERVISOR TRAINING

Managers, supervisors, human resource personnel, and security professionals need training on proper threat identification and intervention techniques. When employees come to management to voice concerns over the behavior of another employee, management personnel must have the knowledge and resources to handle the situation. Policies and procedures on dealing with potentially violent employees and customers should be available, and all managers and supervisors must be thoroughly familiar with these written programs.

Not only must managers and supervisors be able to respond to employee concerns, they must also be able to identify situations that put them at personal risk. In a significant number of violent workplace incidents, employees or former employees return to the work site to get revenge on the person that they believe wronged them. Many times, the "wrongdoer" is the person who disciplined or terminated the employee —that is, the manager, supervisor, human resource manager, or union steward.

Managers must know when to contact the crisis intervention team or local law enforcement personnel. The first report of suspicious behavior is usually channeled through the frontline supervisors. A manager or supervisor may be the first person on the scene when an employee, customer, or client becomes enraged. Managers and supervisors require specific training to guide them through the crisis. When the situation is controllable, the manager or supervisor must be proficient at defusing aggressive behavior before hostility escalates. This includes knowing the warning signs that usually precipitate violent behavior. (They are discussed in Chapter 7.)

If violence does erupt, managers, supervisors, and employees need to know evacuation and other procedures. Who will be responsible for ensuring all employees are accounted for, and how will they do this? As in a fire, employees must be accounted for after an act of workplace violence, and a search must be conducted for those who are missing. Such procedures must be established, documented, and trained for in advance.

Managers and supervisors must also understand the legal requirements for providing a safe and secure work environment for all employees. They could be held liable for their decisions.

Training should be conducted to educate hiring personnel, including managers and supervisors, about preemployment screening and background checks for new employees. A negligent hiring lawsuit could easily result when the wrong employee is put into a position of trust without the proper background screening. Negligent hiring and negligent retention is covered in Chapter 6. The procedures for referring employees to available assistance programs should be included in managerial training and in the policies and procedures manual. With proper referrals to counseling services, many potential problems can be resolved before they become critical or dangerous.

CRISIS INTERVENTION TEAM TRAINING

The crisis intervention team should be composed of the following professionals: the human resource or employee relations manager, the security manager, a psychiatrist or psychologist, an attorney who specializes in labor law, and, if applicable, a union representative. Each member of the team offers specialized expertise. The combination of each person's knowledge and experience should put the team in a good position to carry out the responsibilities associated with crisis intervention.

At least one person on the intervention team, perhaps the security manager, should be trained on all topics taught to employees, supervisors, and managers. The team must know the extent of the information and training available to the rest of the company.

The three main goals of the team are to:

1. Gather and document information regarding the incident, threat, or behavior being investigated.

2. Analyze the information gathered.

3. Recommend a course of action to the decision makers.

Each person on the team should provide input into the evaluation and recommendations. By working together as a team, the group can develop action plans to resolve crises before tragedy strikes. In the event that workplace violence does occur, the team will also be instrumental in the recovery process. Each team member should be trained in his or her role in the business recovery plan.

Training Topics

Employee Training

- Security awareness

- Overview of workplace violence

- Internal and external threats

- Signs of potentially violent behavior

- Robbery procedures and prevention measures

- Location and operation of alarm equipment

- Access-control measures and ID badges

- Reporting requirements and procedures

- Company policies and procedures

- Whom to call for help

- Availability of security and police

Supervisor and Manager Training

Supervisor and manager training consists of all of the topics included in the employee training, plus the following:

- Pre-employment screening practices

- Employee-assistance programs

- Emergency response and evacuation procedures

- Behavioral observation

- Patterns of behavior

- Defusing volatile situations

- Employee adverse reaction training

- Acting and reacting to employee behavior

- Legal requirements and labor relations

Crisis Intervention Team Training

At least one team member should study all the above topics. The rest of the team members need training in the following:

- Threat evaluation and response

- Team effectiveness

- Business recovery planning

HIRING

As the old computer saying goes, "Garbage in, garbage out." The same concept holds true for the work force. Proper screening, testing, and hiring policies and procedures should be in place to ensure that the best candidate is hired to fill an open position. Not only is this good security sense; it's also good business sense. (See the box "Good Hiring Practices.")

Proper screening and background checks on new employees can prevent workplace violence. Fill an open position in your company as you would fill a child-care position in your home. You would never bring a total stranger into your home and leave him or her unsupervised with your baby. The same should hold true for your business. Yet hundreds of times every day across the United States, people hire employees to begin jobs based solely on the information provided on a job application.

Research indicates that one-third of all job applicants falsify their employment applications.[1] These falsifications include everything imaginable. Some applicants make up college degrees and employment experience to increase their chances of obtaining a position. Some alter or omit felony convictions, job terminations, and even social security numbers to meet their needs.

If you were hiring a person to baby-sit your child, you would use every caution and verify the applicant's credibility and credentials before you gave away the key to the house. You would contact the former employers, and you might even drive by the applicant's home to see if it is clean and cared for. You might require the potential child-care provider to produce copies of insurance papers, a driver's license, state certificates, and copies of first aid or cardiopulmonary resuscitation (CPR) certifications. Once you are convinced that the baby-sitter is an honest and reputable person, you might hire him or her on a trial basis until you feel even more certain of the baby-sitter's credentials.

Many businesses don't use the same precautions when filling open positions. Laws vary from state to state on the methods employers can use to conduct background checks on applicants. Some states restrict background investigations until after a person has actually been hired to fill a position. If it is discovered that the applicant falsified the employment application, he or she can be terminated. As an employer, you should know the laws for your state before deciding on the hiring practices you will use. Invasion of privacy can be a costly mistake for your company. Your options may include honesty tests, polygraph tests, criminal checks, and in some cases, credit checks.

Negligent hiring can also be a costly mistake. Negligent hiring is a legal doctrine that holds that the employer may be held liable when they fail to use reasonable care in choosing an applicant, given the risks associated with the position to be filled. The theory behind this doctrine is that the company must determine—before hiring—that the applicant is not a risk to others given the scope of the position. The employer must check the applicant's background to determine if there is reason to believe that the applicant would be unacceptable for the position.

To illustrate, suppose again that you need to hire a baby-sitter to care for your young child. A candidate who has been convicted of child endangerment or child abuse is probably not somebody that you would trust to be alone with your child. Failing to uncover the candidate's history of child endangerment or abuse could be considered negligent hiring. If another candidate had been found guilty of tax evasion, this may or may not affect your hiring decision—unless the applicant was applying for a tax audit position.

Different positions entail different risks. The position of security officer involves a different set of risks than the position of cafeteria attendant. The position of security officer at a gated community involves different risks than the same position at a nuclear facility. When attempting to determine the risks associated with a position, consider the types of access that the employee has. Will the employee have access to master keys, weapons, vulnerable individuals, private homes, drugs, or other items that require special precautions? Imagine for a moment the potential damage that could be caused by a drug addict acting irresponsibly in a nuclear power plant. Background checks for positions in nuclear power plants must be thorough. The damages resulting from negligent hiring could affect millions of people. Don't we, as citizens, have an expectation that the people who are filling these positions are diligent in conducting background checks?

Other positions requiring special consideration are jobs that require the employee to enter another person's home. Examples of these jobs include repair technicians, meter readers, visiting nurses, apartment complex managers, and service workers such as police officers. People who open their doors to admit a company's representative trust that the company has already taken their safety into consideration when hiring the employee. People who unlock their doors for your employee have a right to expect that the employee will act within the boundaries of both the law and the company's policies.

The abundance of laws protecting applicants from invasion of privacy place the employer in a catch-22 situation. As the employer, you must use reasonable care and conduct background checks before hiring an applicant, yet you must be careful in how you conduct these preemployment checks.

Employers are typically very guarded in the information they are willing to provide about former employees because they wish to stay out of court. A very thin line exists between what an employer can and can't, should and shouldn't, do. There are, however, legal ways to conduct checks without the danger of litigation. Check with your legal counsel before beginning a background check.

There are numerous ways to check up on applicants to determine whether they have falsified their job application and whether they are telling the truth about their general history. The depth of the preemployment investigation should depend on the duties of the position and the risks related to that position.

Good Hiring Practices

- Ask current employees for recommendations for vacant positions.

- Have each applicant fill out and sign a formal job application.

- Ask for the names, addresses and phone numbers of former employers.

- Request written permission to contact former employers.

- Request written permission to check academic records.

- Question periods of unemployment and declining salaries.

- Prepare well for the interview.

- Ask behavioral questions (that is, " Describe a time when you....").

- Check personal and professional references.

- Conduct background checks on criminal convictions, driving record, and credit, if applicable.

- Do not ask questions that may be illegal (i.e., age, marital status, religion, sexual preferences).

THE APPLCATION FORM AND RESUME

The place to start the screening process is with the application for employment. Every business should use an application form that asks about the applicant's level of education and previous employment. When screening the applicant, investigate periods of unexplained unemployment.

Some applicants leave the job market for perfectly legitimate reasons. Some parents decide to stay home and care for their children. It's also becoming more common for people to stay home and care for elderly parents or relatives who need constant care. Whatever the case, the applicant should be able to provide a solid reason for the period of unemployment.

When the unemployment cannot be explained, there is cause for concern. During the unexplained period of time, did the applicant obtain money illegally, spend time in jail, or fulfill a community service sentencing? Perhaps the applicant didn't work because of laziness or drug or alcohol abuse. If the reason for leaving the job market is valid, the applicant should be willing and able to explain it.

The application form should request information regarding the applicant's prior job and salary history for at least the past ten years. Applicants who jump from job to job will likely not last long at your company. Emotional problems may be a reason why the applicant was unable to retain any position for an extended period of time.

For each position held, applicants should be asked why they left the company, and they should be asked for permission to contact the former supervisor. Applicants who say they left a former position due to a personality conflict or an inability to get along with management may be signaling that they lack people skills. Ask open-ended questions to probe for more exact details.

Also look at the applicant's salary history. A history of declining salaries should also raise a red flag. Tactfully ask the applicant why he or she is looking for a lower position (or responsibility level) than held before. Investigate the possibility that the applicant may have a condition that diminishes reliability or productivity over time. It could be a chronic condition such as muscular dystrophy or it could be drug or alcohol abuse. Whatever the reason, the applicant should be able to provide and explanation for the decline in salary over the years.

The application form should ask for information about the applicant's educational background. In addition to the schools and colleges attended, applicants should provide the address, telephone number, and dates of attendance for each school. Areas of study, grades, and special activities should also be listed.

For technical or higher-level positions, the hiring decision often rests, at least in part, on the applicant's scholastic achievements. Exaggerating scholastic achievements is common. Ask applicants to provide an official transcript from each college. The majority of colleges use a seal to mark transcripts as official. A seal that indents the paper, similar to a notary stamp, reduces the applicant's ability to change the grades and then photocopy the result. Contact the registrar's office at all colleges that the applicant attended to find out about the type of stamp used on official transcripts.

Carefully compare the information on the transcripts against the information provided on the application form and resume. All applicants want to look their best, and some overstate their grades slightly. Rounding grade point averages up a tenth of a percent is typical. Depending on the position, this embellishment might be disregarded. Some applicants may not remember their exact grade point average and will write down what they think it was. When the numbers are close and there are no other reasons to suspect dishonesty, a simple explanation from the applicant should suffice.

When a significant discrepancy is present or when other issues of honesty are involved, look closer at the applicant's history and background. If there are major discrepancies, remove the applicant from the list of applicants. For example, an applicant who claims to have a college degree but did not finish college should be dropped from consideration.

When you believe that somebody may have falsified the application or resume, you may want to request a second application. Have the person fill out the second form without referring to any records. Explain that you understand the applicant might not remember exact dates, addresses, or telephone numbers. The information on the second application will be less detailed than on the first application. This should be expected. When you compare the two applications and the resume, look for major flaws and omissions.

Every application form should advise the applicant that falsifying information is grounds for immediate termination of employment. Request written permission to contact former employers and conduct a background check to verify information contained on the application. Make sure the applicant signs the application form.

THE INTERVIEW

The interview process is designed to discover whether the applicant is qualified and suited for the position available. When the interview is conducted correctly, it provides the interviewer with the opportunity to learn more about the applicant. It also gives the applicant a chance to answer any questions raised about the application form.

Preparation is the key to a successful interview. Take time before the interview to review the duties and the responsibilities of the position; look over the job description, if available. Then prepare a set of written questions related to the performance of the job. All questions asked should directly correlate to the position for which the applicant is being interviewed. Obviously, questions about religion, age, marital status, and the like are illegal and may cause legal problems for the interviewer and the company later.

Take the written list of questions into the interview with you. When writing out the questions, leave plenty of space between them to allow you to take notes. The list will help you stay on track during the interview and will help you avoid questions that may be illegal.

When you meet with the applicant, shake hands and introduce yourself. Help the applicant feel comfortable by breaking the initial tension with small talk about the weather or traffic. You want the applicant to be as comfortable as possible in order to gain a realistic opinion of how the person would operate in the work environment.

A relatively new concept in interviewing involves examining how the applicant behaved in the past. The interviewer asks questions that require the applicant to describe his or her own experiences. This leads away from the typical question-and-answer period that all college seniors study during Interviewing Concepts 101 class. We have all been through the interviews in which we were questioned about our biggest fault. The standard answer for that, of course, " I'm far too dedicated to my job, and I work much, much too hard." The interviewee would never give an honest answer. For example, although my biggest fault is that I like to stare out the window a lot, I would not give that as an answer.

Behavioral interviewing focuses more directly on how the applicant actually behaved in the past. The questions begin with some sort of pretext like the following:

- Tell me of a time when you...

- Give me an example of when you...

- How did you handle...

- When you were presented with ...

- Before, when you had a problem with...

The questions can be modified to elicit a behavioral response indicating how the applicant reacted to a similar set of circumstances in the past. For example, you might say, "Tell me of a time when you and your supervisor had a major disagreement about how a task should be handled." Don't let applicants who claim that they've never disagreed with the boss off the hook. We all know that's impossible!

As an interviewer, you want to know how applicants handled this matter before and get an idea of what to expect from them in the future. Most people have had more than one disagreement with a former employer. Applicants' answers may reflect the most significant or trying episode that they have ever had. How the applicant answers this question may be the key to how this person handles frustration.

If the applicant has initial difficulty answering this question or any other, you can always go back and ask the same question later. The answer is important and definitely worth the wait. The person you hire may stick with the company for many years, and you want to choose wisely.

Take plenty of notes during the interview, and ensure that your notes would stand up in a court of law. Don't take notes on physical appearance or other matters that are expressly prohibited by law. It is good practice to offer the interviewee the option to review the notes that have been taken. Most applicants will pass up the opportunity. Your notes will assist you later in the decision-making process. It will also help refresh you memory when differentiating between numerous applicants.

THE BACKGROUND CHECK

After the interview has taken place and the candidate list has been narrowed down to one to three people, it's time to start verifying the information provided on the application or resume and given during the interview. The extent of the background check you perform depends on the type of position to be filled.

At a minimum, check with former employers. Due to the possibility of lawsuits, most companies limit the information they supply about former employees to the dates of employment and possibly the beginning and ending wages. Some companies do provide additional information so it's worth the effort to ask.

Ask the applicant to list at least three personal and professional references and to provide written approval to contact them. The human resources staff should definitely contact these people. Previous supervisors should also be contacted for reference information. When calling for references, have a list of questions ready and take notes. Ask about statements and incidents that the candidate described during the interview. For example, suppose you asked the applicant, "Tell me of a time when you had two important deadlines due at the same time and you only had enough time to complete one project. How did you handle this?" Suppose the applicant responded,

> Project X and the annual sales figures were both due at three o'clock. At one o'clock, when I realized there was no way to turn them both in on time, I went to my supervisor and let him decide which project should take priority.

Ask the supervisor about that specific incident to determine whether the applicant was honest in describing the incident during the interview. Ask the former supervisor if he would hire the employee again if given the opportunity. He will probably say yes to avoid potential hassles later on. Listen to the tone of his voice, and listen for any signs of hesitation that might indicate a less than honest answer.

TERMINATION

When disciplinary measures fail to provide the necessary results and an employee's unacceptable behavior continues, it is time to terminate the employee. Most managers and supervisors find this aspect of the job one of the hardest to accomplish. When the difficulty of the termination is compounded by the threat of violence from the employee, it becomes much harder.

Regardless of the reason for the termination, the manager, supervisor, and the human resources professional must do their homework in advance. Preparation is a key principle when terminating an employee. Knowing in advance that all of the *i*'s are dotted and the *t*'s are crossed will assist you when you call the employee in for that fateful meeting. Not only will preparation help keep you out of court, but it will help you sleep better at night, knowing that the termination was fully justified.

Fired employees often say that it was not the fact that they were terminated that upset them, but the way the termination was handled. Terminations are never pleasant experiences for either party, but respect and consideration are essential. (See the box "Good Termination Practices.")

When you fire an employee, you should expect some type of emotional response. Such reactions are expected and normal. These include anger, frustration, disbelief, depression, denial, and hysteria. The employee may move from one emotional outburst to another in a matter of minutes. The range of the emotion may change rapidly and with little notice.

Plan the termination in advance, and prepare all documentation. If human resource professionals are available, they should review the termination package to ensure the termination is legal and that all the paperwork is in order. If you suspect that the employee may become violent, notify the security department before the termination meeting. (Additional information on this is provided in Chapter 7.)

Always conduct the termination in a private location, and keep the meeting brief. Tell the employee up front that he or she is being terminated—and why. If the company policy dictates that the employee receive a termination letter, provide it right away. Keep the termination letter brief and to the point. If the employee will receive any severance benefits, present this information in writing during the meeting.

Termination should be conducted late in the business day. After the termination, do not allow the employee to return to the work area without an escort. A security officer, supervisor, or manager may want to escort the person back to the work area to collect personal belongings. In some companies, the supervisor or manager cleans out the employee's desk and takes any personal belonging to the room where the termination is taking place. The employee is given the opportunity to review the items to see if anything has been overlooked.

During the termination meeting, ask the employee to turn over all keys, access cards, identification badges, company credit cards, cell phones, and any other company property. If the employee had access to voice mail systems, computer systems, or access systems, access privileges should be deactivated immediately. When keys are not returned, the doors should be re-keyed to prevent access into the facility. The employee should also be told that he or she is not allowed back onto company property without a prior written appointment with the human resources manager or the business owner. Pass-codes to cylinder locks should also be changed.

Do not subject the terminated employee to the embarrassment of being escorted from the building in front of former coworkers or customers. The employee may specifically ask to remain until most of the people have left the building. This request should be granted when feasible.

When the threat of violence is a real possibility, the company can seek a court-issued injunction barring the employee from company property. This injunction can be expanded to help protect those who were instrumental in the employee's termination. An injunction should not be viewed as a cure-all for security measures, however. The former employee may become enraged when served with an injunction. It may intensify his or her anger and make retaliation a more genuine possibility. However, in many jurisdictions the injunction will assist law enforcement officers who intervene during a trespass incident.

The receptionist must be informed of the termination and of any possibility of danger that may exist. A picture of the employee should be placed where the receptionist and any other employees near open-access doors can see it. Showing a picture once and then taking it away will only be as effective as the receptionist's memory. The picture should not be displayed where all employees can see it, unless it is a very volatile situation. I've seen termination booklets where the pictures are posted and any additional information is noted. Receptionists and security officers often initial next to the picture to indicate they have received the notice of termination. Pictures of people other than employees who pose a threat can be included in this notebook (i.e.: customers that are barred, estranged spouses, people who have been previously removed from the property).

Employees sitting near open-access points do not need to know the reason for the termination; only that a significant threat has been made. Information on threats must be communicated to employees who are in access-controlled areas. Receptionists and other employees need to know whether the threat involves guns, knives, or other weapons. The failure to provide this information puts the affected employees in a risky position, and the failure to disclose this risk could land the business in a lawsuit if violence occurs.

Additional security protection should be provided for the supervisor, manager, and human resources people who were involved in the termination. This may include walking them to and from their cars, monitoring their visitors and deliveries, and perhaps even providing security recommendations for their homes.

Even when an employee's identification badge has been returned and all the access privileges have been canceled, caution should still be exercised. On December 7, 1988, David Burke, a discharged airline employee, boarded a plane scheduled to fly from Los Angeles to San Francisco. He used his employee identification badge to bypass security at the airport. Burke shot his former boss during the flight, then went to the cockpit and shot both the pilot and the copilot. The plane crashed, killing all forty-three people on board. The airline claims that it did receive Burke's identification badge when it terminated his employment, but it was possible for an employee to have more than one badge.

Good Termination Practices

- Complete all documentation in advance.

- Have the human resource department review the termination package.

- Conduct all terminations in private, near the end of the business day.

- Alert security officers prior to the meeting.

- Keep termination meetings brief.

- Retrieve all identification badges, keys, company credit cards, cell phones, beepers, and all other company property.

- Cancel computer, voice mail, E-mail, and any other electronic access privileges.

- Notify employees who need to know (receptionists, etc.).

- Provide additional security for supervisors, managers, and human resource personnel who assisted with the termination.

EMPLOYEE-ASSISTANCE PROGRAMS (EAPs)

Employee-assistance programs were first developed in the 1940s to help employees who were dealing with alcohol abuse. Often, employers designated employees who successfully recovered from alcohol addiction as on-site counseling representatives. They provided support and help to other employees with alcohol addiction. When problem employees became too much of a nuisance for the employer to deal with and the in-house counseling failed, they were simply fired and replaced.

As time went on, employers began to understand that discharging problem employees was not an effective or cost-efficient solution. The emergence of labor unionization, termination polices, and increased termination litigation forced U.S. business and industry to develop a more proactive and economical manner to salvage employees who would have otherwise been fired.

The first modern employee-assistance programs (EAPs) varied in form and technique. Some management philosophies dictated a "fix it or be fired" approach. The employee was formally put on notice that management knew a problem existed, and he or she was warned that continued employment was contingent on the problem being immediately corrected. For employees already facing problems, this do-it-or-die approach was of little value. It didn't take long for these EAP counselors to gain a reputation as the grim reapers of employment.

As time when on, business professionals learned that employee problems had an even larger and more significant impact on the company's profits than they had suspected. Employees were bringing more problems to work with them than alcohol- and drug-related difficulties. Studies showed that a work force suffering from stress caused by a multitude of emotional problems costs companies huge amounts of money. The company's survival could be determined by the mental well-being of the workers.

Today's EAPs were developed to help management reduce the costs associated with increased tardiness, absenteeism, sick time, rising health-care and worker's compensation expenses, and other costs related to poor job performance. Throughout the years, the role of EAPs has evolved to encompass more of the problems that workers face, including substance abuse, uncontrolled stress, family and marital problems, and employment-related difficulties. In the counseling role, the recovering alcoholic was replaced with clinical professionals in the fields of social work, psychology, and counseling.

Three main types of EAPs exist today: telephonic, in-house, and purchased services. In the first type of service, employees are given a toll free number whenever they want to receive assistance. The telephone is answered by a counselor who makes an initial assessment of the employee's problem and refers the employee to a local agency that contracts with the national EAP. Telephonic services are often the least expensive and least effective programs available. I had an employee tell me once they called the toll free number when they felt seriously suicidal. The toll free number was widely posted at her employer's work-site and advertised as a "great resource." The caller was told by the EAP person who answered the phone that there were no counselors available and to try back on Monday morning. The people paid to care about and counsel her told her that not even they cared. The lady never did call back on Monday morning. Luckily, she had a more reliable place to turn to during her crisis.

Many large companies have begun to provide employees with in-house EAP services. They retain a trained professional staff on location, and these counselors work very closely with both the management and the employees on problem resolution. Many of the companies that have switched to this type of program have experienced tremendous success. Unfortunately, small and medium-size companies do not have the resources to offer an in-house EAP.

The last type of EAP is purchased services. With purchased services, the company contracts with a mental-health provider in the local area to furnish EAP services. Employers generally have a choice in paying a flat fee per year per employee or paying for the actual services as they are used. The type of program set-up typically depends on the needs of the company. Purchased services are often the best option for companies that want to contract for employee-assistance counseling.

A relatively new concept in employee-assistance programs employs corporate chaplains or other members of the clergy as counselors. This practice has been widely used in the military and in hospitals. Many large corporations are also using clergy services to assist employees with problems and to assist management in defusing potential volatile situations. Substantial growth in this field is expected as more corporations discover the value of providing these services to their employees.

The type of EAP service obtained depends on the company's management philosophy, the level of employee need, and the company's financial resources. Small businesses and companies with limited financial resources may elect to join forces with other companies in the same position and negotiate a shared contract for services.

The two main objectives of any EAP are to help employees resolve problems that affect their well-being and to turn problem employees into productive employees in a cost-efficient manner. It is far less expensive to rehabilitate an employee with poor performance due to life pressures than to interview, hire and train a new worker.

Federal laws protect employees with certain physical and mental disorders. The Americans with Disabilities Act (ADA) requires employers to make reasonable accommodations for workers with handicaps. In many cases, the employer must also make accommodations for employees who are suffering from mental illness. A major implication of this law is that employers now have a duty to assist in rehabilitating mentally ill employees.

I interviewed Dr. Barbara Murphy to gain her insight into the role that EAPs play in business and industry. Dr. Murphy is the Mental Health Director at Allen Memorial Hospital in Waterloo, Iowa. In addition to other duties, she manages the hospital's EAP purchased-services program. Much of this section reflects Dr. Murphy's observations and recommendations regarding the role of EAPs in the overall well-being of workers and the reduction of employee violence.

According to Dr. Murphy, a key factor in developing and maintaining a useful EAP depends on employees taking advantage of the services. Having a wonderful in-house EAP staffed by professional counselors and others from the mental-health community will be a severe waste of time, money, and talent if employees do not utilize the program.

Employees sometimes fail to take advantage of the services provided by EAPs because they are unfamiliar with the program or believe it to be ineffective. This first roadblock—lack of familiarity with the program—can be resolved by the company's human resource professionals or management personnel who make a commitment to the well-being of employees. Take advantage of all opportunities to inform employees about the EAP services. There are a number of inexpensive ways to educate and remind employees about the assistance services available, including pamphlets enclosed with paychecks, posters, articles in the company newsletter, and a descriptive summary of services in the benefits manual. Presentations during lunch periods, commonly known as lunch-and-learns or brown-bag lunches also serve as a tool for company education.

The EAP representatives should also actively advertise themselves to employees. They should make a very strong effort to make their services known to employees. They can make themselves more visible through seminars on topics of interest to workers, such as stress reduction, conflict resolution, and marriage and family services. These classes will also increase the rapport between workers and the EAP staff. Later, if the employee is considering using the EAP, already being familiar with the staff makes picking up the telephone a bit easier.

Overcoming employees' perceptions that the program is ineffective is more difficult. The first step toward resolving this problem is to find out from employees why they are not using the program. Determining the areas of employee concern with the program will help management and human resources personnel determine what steps are needed to ensure employee confidence in the program. If employees feel that the EAP is not effective, management may need to look for a different service provider.

Employees may perceive a lack in confidentiality with the in-house or outside program administrators. Employees generally do not want their personal weaknesses or problems to be the topic of discussion at every table in the company cafeteria. Employees who do not believe their cases will be handled in a confidential manner will not seek assistance through these resources.

The timeliness of services is another reason why employees fail to use EAP services. The assistance program will not work for employees who must wait several weeks for an appointment. According to Dr. Murphy, "It has been proven that people will not wait to resolve a crisis. People who wait six weeks before an appointment will resolve their crisis in another way. Unfortunately, sometimes they do it with a gun." The timeliness of services is thus a very relevant issue. Recall the suicidal woman who called the EAP only to be told to call back on Monday morning? As with so many other things in life, timing is everything.

For employees who display the warning signs of violent behavior, an initial assessment by a mental-health professional must be made as soon as possible. The assessment should take place no more than 24 hours after the initial referral. In almost every incident of employee violence in the workplace, the employee displayed clear warning signs of violent behavior. Many employees flatly told their supervisors of their intentions, then followed through with their threats. These types of incidents can often be prevented. According to Dr. Murphy, employers who ignore employee threats are courting disaster.

When employees who are frustrated believe that they are not being taken seriously and are asked to wait for counseling services, the waiting period only reinforces their feelings of anger and frustration. Some employees decide to show their employer just how serious they are. The results of this type of display are never beneficial to any of the people involved.

Dr. Murphy suggests several reasons why supervisors, managers, and coworkers ignore the threats of angry employees. Most people can't even imagine using a gun to solve their problems. When a coworker threatens violence, others don't think the threat is real. It's easier to think that the employee is just blowing off steam or venting frustrations. Even worse, coworkers sometimes ignore the threats because "it's just old Joe, and he's been saying that for years."

In some, if not all, states, the employer has the right to demand that an employee seek help from an EAP as a condition of continued employment. Employers considering making a mandatory referral should check with legal counsel to verify their rights. A mandatory referral should not be used in place of other disciplinary actions. All actions should be based on job performance.

Once an employee receives a mandatory referral to an EAP, the counselor should work with the employee and the supervisor to achieve the goals required for continued employment. According to Dr. Murphy, the first thing a counselor should do is ask the referred employee to sign a release of information form.

Rules of confidentiality are very strict, and the information that the counselor is entitled to provide to anyone is restricted. The employer may request the counselor to tell the employer whether the employee showed up for an appointment, arrived on time, and actively participated in the session. The EAP counselor cannot discuss the specifics of the conversation with the employer, nor can the counselor disclose the recommendations given to the employee. The counselor's role is that of an advocate for the employee. The counselor's loyalty must be to the employee, not the employer, regardless of who pays the bill.

However, the scope of confidentiality does not cover genuine threats made against others, according to Dr. Murphy. A counselor or psychiatrist who determines that an employee is dangerous to others must inform the target of the threats and the local police department. If the counselor believes that a supervisor, manager, or other employee is in danger, the counselor must notify this person. Some state laws vary slightly, but this is a widely accepted legal practice. The security and human resources departments will not be notified by the EAP professional unless department personnel are the potential victims. However, the targeted employee may report the threat to one or more of these departments.

If the counselor determines that the danger is directed toward the employee's spouse, he or she should be warned, not the employer. It is mandatory that all counselors, doctors, psychiatrists, and nurses report suspected child abuse. If the counselor has reasonable suspicion that an employee is abusing a child, the counselor must report the incident to law enforcement officials.

In cases in which the employee needs counseling but is not a threat to the safety of others, the counselor will begin treatment for the employee. Most EAPs are designed to offer only short-term treatment. The EAP counselor will typically see the employee for one to six sessions, depending on the nature of the problem. This type of counseling approach is often referred to as *problem focused*. During the initial counseling session, the counselor assesses the situation and determines in what areas the employee needs assistance. The counselor then moves into a problem-solving mode to help the employee develop an action plan for resolution.

According to Dr. Murphy, it is sometimes readily apparent that the employee needs long-term help that the EAP is not designed to provide. In this case, the counselor tries to convince the employee that a problem exists. The EAP professional tries to break down any resistance that the employee may have toward treatment. The counselor tries to show the employee that with additional help, the situation can be resolved or improved. This is the case when the employee is involved in an abusive situation or is dealing with drug- or alcohol-related problems.

In some situations, the counselor may believe that the employee's problems are caused by a medical condition. In this case, the counselor refers the employee to a physician for evaluation and treatment. When the employee decides to undergo treatment, the EAP professional works with the health-care provider to ensure that the referral is covered by the employee's medical policy. If the employee does not have medical coverage, the EAP counselor tries to refer the employee to a local agency that provides services on a sliding-fee basis. Whatever the nature or origin of an employee's problems, the EAP professional's goal is to assist the employee in becoming a fully productive and stable person again.

Dr. Murphy suggests that in cases in which the job or the supervisor is the source of the employee's problems, the counselor may recommend that the employee consider transferring to another department or evaluating other employment opportunities. The counselor should help the employee explore all options. The counselor should never advise clients on a course of action. Instead, the counselor should help them identify the options that best serve their needs. In a situation like this, a transfer or new job is probably best for the employer as well. The employer will be better off without an angry or disgruntled employee.

Dr. Murphy recommends that all employers who offer an EAP survey their employees to find out how they view the program and whether or not, if they had the need, they would take advantage of EAP services. "An EAP is not a good deal if it doesn't do anything. Just like anything else, if it's on sale and you don't need it and it doesn't do anything for you, it's no sale." Shop around before contracting with an EAP agency.

The EAP profession has grown rapidly, and not all service providers who bid on a contract are equipped to provide the services that a company and its employees need. Dr. Murphy encourages employers who are considering contracting for EAP services to ask the following questions:

1. Is the EAP agency familiar with local conditions and local service providers?

2. Does the agency have experience with similar companies and similar employees?

3. Can the agency provide letters of recommendation?

4. What type of paperwork can the company expect to receive from the agency, and what is the frequency of reporting (monthly, quarterly, annually)?

5. Can the agency provide in-house training, and if so, what types of training programs can they provide?

6. Does the agency provide a twenty-four-hour crisis line?

7. What range of providers does the agency work with?

8. What is the cost of the agency's services?

9. Does the agency work with insurance carriers on referrals?

INTERVENTION AND ACTION PLANS

As discussed earlier, every company should have a written policy that reflects a no-tolerance level for harassment, intimidation, threats, or violence of any kind against employees, customers, or visitors. Written guidelines must exist to assist supervisors and managers in confronting and resolving perceived and real conflicts. In large corporations, a specialized team may be available to handle the intervention process. In small businesses, the owner or manager may be the only immediate resource available to employees who feel threatened. Whatever the case, knowing and deciding in advance which actions are necessary to deal with potential problems will help speed up resolution with minimal disruption of operations.

The initial notice of a potential problem will most likely come from a concerned or threatened employee. One or more employees may notify management when they believe that the actions of a disgruntled employee are no longer tolerable. The employees will likely have been dealing with this employee for a long time and are no longer willing to handle the situation themselves. Employees often hesitate before reporting an incident. They may believe they are overreacting to the disgruntled employee, or they may not want to cause the employee additional problems. Regardless of the reason for waiting before filing a complaint, care should be used not to discourage the employees. Their hesitation is based on concerns that are real to them.

Education is one of the best tools management can use to diminish the risks of workplace violence. All employees—from the factory welder to the supervisor—must know how to recognize a coworker who is an explosion waiting to happen. Employees must also feel comfortable reporting incidents and individuals to management without the fear of reprisal from either the dysfunctional employee or management staff. In some large companies, the human resources department has a hot line or voice mail system through which concerned employees can leave anonymous messages.

In today's workplace, where everybody seems to have to do more with less, managers and supervisors may feel perturbed at having to investigate a harassment or intimidation claim. They may feel from the beginning that even if a significant concern is warranted, human resources or another department may sweep the entire incident under the rug without ever confronting the employee. They may believe that any investigation on their part is an exercise in futility and that the investigation and investment of their time and resources would be wasted.

Employees who sense these types of feelings, or have actually found this to be the case in the past, will be reluctant to voice concerns about another employee's behavior. When a single employee or group of employees feels threatened, immediate action must be taken to resolve the situation, or valued employees will themselves become increasingly unproductive or quit their jobs out of fear for their safety and well-being.

All cases reported to management must be fully investigated in a timely manner. The reporting employees should be treated with respect and consideration during the investigation. Once a threat is reported, the team responsible for threat evaluation and intervention should meet. The members of this team may include the human resources manager, the security manager, the employee's manager or supervisor, union representation, EAP professionals, a psychologist, and in some cases, local law enforcement officials. The size of the team depends on the resources available to the business. In large companies, all of these people may be available but called only after the initial evaluation has been completed.

In smaller businesses, security, human resources, and EAP representatives may not be available. The owner/manager should consider contracting outside agencies for assistance with the evaluation. When local law enforcement officials are informed of a problem, the company must take responsibility for ensuring that the responding officers understand the urgency of the situation.

The responding agency must know all of the facts involved; not just what the company wants to disclose. Some companies feel a need to protect the employee's privacy for fear of causing additional problems for both the employee and the company by bringing in an outside agency. Once a threat has been made, however, secrecy almost becomes a moot point. Because an arrest may not always be made after the first incident, the local police officials must at least document the incident. The documented history will assist both the company and law enforcement officials if additional incidents occur.

Not all response team members need to be experts, but they do need to be trained in identifying, evaluating, and dealing with aggressive behaviors. All team members must be familiar with the company policy on intimidating behavior and the company's intervention and action plan for dealing with threats of violence or harassment.

Once a report has been made, the response team interviews the person who came forward to determine the exact circumstances in which the threat or behavior occurred. When a verbal threat is involved, the exact wording of the threat can be an important indicator of the employee's intention. The team can also determine whether this was an isolated or ongoing event. When a history of past incidents exists, record as many details as possible but concentrate on the latest or most significant incident.

Ask for the names of witnesses or others that may have knowledge of the incident being reported. The reporting employee may be reluctant to provide a list of other employees for fear of his or her identity (or the complaint itself) becoming known. Reassure the employee that all conversations and interviews will remain confidential. To assist in maintaining confidentiality, conduct all meetings away from the immediate work area. If the building is small or privacy is not readily available, conduct all interviews away from the work site.

Determine whether the threat was aimed at the reporting employee, another worker, a manager or supervisor, or the company as a whole. Ask the reporting employee about his or her relationship with the disgruntled employee, especially if the threat was aimed directly at the reporting party. If it becomes apparent that the two employees had a romantic relationship before the threat and that the relationship is the cornerstone of the threat, intervention is still required. You cannot dismiss the issue as being a personal or civil matter. The workplace is now involved, and therefore, so is the safety of all employees. Ignoring a seemingly personal problem could be a costly and deadly mistake.

All parts of this interview must be documented. The documentation will aid others who are required to assist in the intervention. It will also be easier to justify disciplinary actions for future incidents when this information is correctly documented on the employee's personnel file. In a worst-case scenario, the documentation can be used as evidence in a future lawsuit. Documentation will show what actions the company took to help resolve the conflict.

Once the initial interview has been completed, the severity of the threat must be determined. If, after an initial interview, there is cause for concern, other witnesses or involved employees should be interviewed. Ideally, the same person should interview all involved employees.

The employee's work history should be examined. Items to pay particular attention to include past situations in which the employee was unable to effectively deal with counseling or coaching. When the employee has a history of violence against family members, coworkers, other people, or animals, extra security measures may be needed to protect the employees being interviewed as well as the interviewer.

Contact local law enforcement officials if the threat is substantiated during the interviews. If law enforcement officials become involved, they may be willing to provide information regarding past arrests or other incidents involving the employee. Some police departments have experts on staff who can help in the evaluation process.

When evaluating the threat, consider the following factors:

- Does the employee have the means to carry out the threat?

- Does the employee have a known history of violent behavior?

- What is the employee's typical behavior?

- What risk factors can be associated with the employee's behavior?

- What other warning signs of violent behavior has the employee exhibited in the past?

Examine the employee's original job application to find out if he or she has a military background. Ask those who are being interviewed whether the investigated employee has been known to carry or own weapons. If they do own or carry weapons, find out what type of weapons they are.

When the intervention team believes the threat to be nothing more than blowing off steam or "talking big" in front of coworkers, the employee must still be counseled about the behavior. Perhaps the employee did not realize the effect of his or her behavior on other people. In this day and age, people lose their sense of humor quickly when they become the recipients of threats.

Security personnel should be made aware of the counseling session in advance. Follow the techniques discussed in Chapter 7 during the meeting with the disgruntled employee. In countless cases of workplace violence, nobody ever talked to the violent employee about his or her behavior before the violent incident. The goal in talking to employees accused of intimidating, harassing, or threatening behavior is to change the behavior. Referral to an EAP or local counseling program may be all that is needed. Such employees need to realize that their future employment depends on their behavior and that they alone are responsible for changing their behavior.

I once talked with a worker fresh out of high school who had used his fingers as a pretend gun. He then used his pistol fingers to point and shoot at others in the cafeteria while saying, "Pow." This, of course, upset the other workers a great deal. Once I told the young gentleman that this was unacceptable behavior, he understood and nothing similar ever happened in the future. He was actually, performance-wise, a superior employee.

According to one expert, "If an employee's threats appear to be a prelude to some more drastic acts of violence, then you can either rehabilitate him or terminate his employment. Rehabilitation means helping the person get his head on straight and come back to work. Often referring the potentially dangerous employee to a traditional employee-assistance counselor is enough. Their behavior may stem from alcoholism or drug abuse, and an EAP counselor can suggest a treatment program that could solve the problem."[2]

During the counseling session, advise the employee being investigated that the company is concerned about his or her behavior and that an investigation is being conducted. Give the employee a copy of the company policy on intimidating and harassing behavior. Ensure that the employee understands the company policy and the relationship between future misconduct and possible termination.

If possible, without revealing the identity of the complaintant, ask the employee for his or her interpretation of the comments or actions under investigation. Give the employee ample time to explain. Listen and take notes. Write down what the employee actually says, not just what you think the employee means. Because taping the conversation involves legal issues that vary from state to state, do not try this before seeking advice from you legal counsel.

When concluding the interview, let the employee know what to expect next. As with any employee counseling session, the employee should leave the room with a clear understanding of what is expected and how long he or she has to achieve these performance objectives. It is always a good idea to provide this list to the employee in writing. A copy should also be kept in the employee's personnel file.

Many companies allow the employee to go home after the meeting. This allows the employee time to think about the discussion and try to make sense out of it. This also affords the employee privacy and keeps him or her away from coworkers. Angry employees sometimes try to recount their side of the story to any employee who is willing to listen. Without a doubt, this results in a disruption of business operations. In addition, the employee who initiated the complaint may feel vulnerable and uncomfortable with the situation. Other employees who support the investigated employee may actually instigate additional threats.

If a very serious or immediate threat is thought to exist, inform security personnel about the meeting, and provide them with enough details so they can respond accordingly. In too many companies managers are so concerned about a breach of confidentiality that they fail to supply pertinent details to people who really have a need to know. Effective security measures can only be initiated when the security department knows exactly what it's dealing with.

Decide on the actions to be followed when a significant danger is present. Will the employee be discharged, and if so, under what conditions? Companies have used various measures to make termination more beneficial and less painful for the employee. Some companies offer the employees large severance packages to leave the company quietly and without conflict. The company must make such decisions independently. Some companies have offered separation packages that include benefits for a given period of time. Normal severance pay and benefits have been extended to help employees feel less angry about their termination. A company that has the means available should offer access to a counseling program and a job-placement referral service. When viable options that may diminish the likelihood of the terminated employee returning violently are available, it may be a wise to exercise them.

SECURITY PROCEDURES

Integrating workplace security policies and practices helps managers reduce the risk of workplace violence. Because not every company can afford, or indeed wants, an armed security guard at every door, the security measures must be broken down into manageable and affordable pieces. The security measures required depend on the actual risk of violence occurring in the workplace.

Risk identification is based on a multitude of factors, each of which must be examined to determine its applicability to the environment in which the business operates. Just as it does not make sense to provide a safe for a child's lemonade stand, it also does not make sense to leave all the doors open at a coin-minting operation.

One of the most beneficial tools for determining the level of risk that a business faces is the security audit. There are many reputable companies that specialize in providing security audit services. For those who lack a background in security, contracting with an auditing agency may be far less expensive and time consuming than trying to complete the audit themselves. The local chamber of commerce should be able to provide guidance in choosing a local firm with a good reputation.

With a comprehensive security audit program, the security manager or another responsible person can analyze areas of potential risk (and potential liability) and compare those risks to the preventative measures in place. The review should look at past incidents of security violations and examine them to calculate both the actual and potential damages from such incidents.

Do not ignore future threats just because they have never occurred before. Identifying the potential for problems is a key factor for preventing problems later. The audit form should also be updated to reflect changes in risk factors as they develop. New businesses or housing developments in the area can significantly change the amount and type of traffic for the company, and hence change the risks involved in doing business in a given area.

The security audit can also be beneficial in determining whether budgeted security dollars are being utilized to their full potential. Risks that were a major concern five years ago may not top the list of priorities today. Just think how a handful of anthrax letters in the fall of 2001 rocked the postal service's world! The budget must be reviewed to ensure that issues of top importance are being addressed. The money spent to provide security services might be better utilized in training employees.

Risks should be examined in relation to the types of people capable of causing the damage. Just as motivations for violence vary, so do the security measures necessary to prevent violence. Violence can erupt from current and former employees, their families, customers, and criminals. Each of these groups must be guarded against with various security measures. Some measures will help protect against all groups, other measures will protect only against one category.

Threats can be broken down into two broad categories: internal and external. (See the box "Types of Threats.") People who are already inside the facility or who gain access without question are considered internal threats. People who must gain entry through the main entrance area or by overcoming physical barriers (such as breaking a window) are considered external threats. Some threats may fall under either category. For example, assault can originate from internal or external sources.

Once the audit has been completed, do not put it into a drawer to collect dust. The audit itself will not correct problem areas. This is where many audits fail. Knowing about possible problems does not prevent the problem from happening. The failure to follow through after an audit could lead to legal problems if employees, customers, or visitors are injured or killed because of a problem that management knew about but did not address. The victims of workplace violence will have an easy case of negligence when they prove that management ignored pertinent security problems.

Resources—both people and funding—should be allocated to correct deficiencies in a manner that produces the greatest reduction in security risks to people. Risks to human life should be addressed before risks of property damage. Property insurance can go a long ways towards restoring a building loss, but there is no policy available to restore a human life.

Threat management tactics can also be divided into two broad categories: internal and external. Sample tactics are listed in the "Threat Management" box. Many of the items listed under "External Threat Management" also apply to managing internal threats.

Types of Threats	
Internal Threats	**External Threats**
Abusive nonviolent employees	Former employees
Disgruntled violent employees	Disgruntled customers
Employee theft	Family members
Employee sabotage	Domestic abuse
Harassment or intimidation	Robberies
Sexual harassment or assault	Bomb threats
Disgruntled vendors	Kidnapping
	Random acts of violence
	Assault/rape
	Terrorism

Threat Management	
Internal Threat Management	**External Threat Management**
Security officers	Security officers
Company policy	Door locks and electronic access
Developed procedures	Duress alarms
Duress alarms	Visitor access controls
Employee training	Closed-circuit television systems
Supervisor/manager training	Fences and gates
Identification badges	Signs and warnings
Human resources support	Registration logs
Employee-assistance programs	Bomb screening equipment
Reporting hot line	Metal detectors
Business recovery planning	Homeland Security Advisory System

ACCESS CONTROL

Physical barriers are among the measures that can be used to prevent external threats from entering the workplace. Examples of external threats include family members, customers, some vendors, and robbers. (Robbery prevention and performance objectives are covered in Part Three.)

Current employees, some vendors, and service contract personnel typically have a wide range of access to most facilities. They often gain admission through side doors with electronic card key access or with a passkey issued by the business. Once they are inside the facility, internal measures are needed to ensure that the security of the facility is maintained. Many of these measures rest with the human resources and security departments.

Photo identification badges should be used to control access by employees, visitors, and guests. The different types of badges vary considerably in price and quality. Temporary tags range from disposable labels to badges that change their physical appearance upon expiration. The latter might expire after a given number of hours or days or even when exposed to direct sunlight. Badge features should be proportional to the amount of risk present.

Every employee should be issued an identification badge on the first day of employment. Badges should be replaced when they become outdated or damaged. Current pictures should always be used. Employees who change their name because of marriage, divorce, or for some other reason should be required to obtain an updated identification badge within a specified period of time, such as 30 days.

Company policy should dictate that the employees wear their badges at all times while in the facility. When only some employees wear their identification badges, the effectiveness of the system is reduced to almost zero. Security officers, supervisors, and managers should be instructed to counsel employees who do not wear their identification badges, and violations of the rule should be dealt with as performance issues.

Information about the employee may be added to the reverse side of the badge. This information can include just about anything the company chooses, such as security color codes, access levels, medical conditions, social security numbers, employee numbers, height, weight, and other physical characteristics. When asking for an employee's weight, be prepared to run into large amounts of resistance. Bar coding this information will offer confidentiality for those who do not want their information visible.

Smaller companies that lack the means to purchase identification badge equipment can consult with local photography studios, which can often produce identification badges at a very reasonable fee. Printing shops can assist in printing the cards used for the badges.

In larger companies, employees should be trained to be cautious with people in the facility who are not wearing identification badges. Identification awareness and procedural training for possible violations should be included in employee training. Intruders should be reported to security personnel without hesitation. The general employee population is not privy to immediate information regarding terminated employees. Just because the company employed a person earlier in the day doesn't mean that he or she is still on the payroll at quitting time.

Employees and others who attempt to gain access to the facility without displaying proper identification should be directed to use the main entrance or whatever entrance the general public uses. The receptionist or security officer on duty should be able to verify employment and issue a temporary identification badge to current employees. When company personnel do not feel comfortable confronting an unauthorized person, they should contact security personnel immediately to report the intruder. Security officers should investigate the unauthorized entry immediately.

Some employees may view the identification badges as a daily hassle, but managers must support and enforce the company policy requiring the badge. The badge itself should be treated as the employee's authorization to enter and remain in the building. I've seen some companies that issue small anniversary pins for various years of service that employees display on their identification badges. The senior employees who wore their pins with pride were a great example to the younger employees. This was a way of increasing employee support for the identification badge system.

A registration book must be present at all doors available for public access. In smaller offices, this would most likely be in the reception area. The sample visitor registration form shown in Figure 6-1 can be modified to meet the specific needs of a location. The extent of information gathered on the registration log depends on the level of security desired. Some companies require that all visitors, vendors, and guests be fingerprinted upon arrival. Although fingerprinting is not essential for visitors at most locations, this example does show how security measures can be instituted to meet the level of risk present.

The registration book requires visitors to supply particular information such as their name, the date, and time of visit, the company they represent (when applicable), and who they are there to see. When escorts are required, they should also write their name in the registration book. When numbered badges are issued, the badge number should also be recorded. Visitors to the facility should be required to sign in and out and to return their visitor badge when leaving the building. They should also be required to leave by the same entrance as they arrived.

The registration log is a permanent record of people entering the building. Pages in the registration log should be removed each day to avoid potential confidentiality issues. Vendors or competitors may try to view the registration log to determine who has been visiting the company.

(COMPANY NAME)

REGISTRATION LOG

Badge #	Date	Name	Company	Time In	Time Out	Escort

Figure 6-1   Sample Registration Log

PHYSICAL SECURITY

Duress, or panic alarms, should be installed in areas where customer or visitor contact occurs. They should be installed in such a way that the employee can activate the alarm without obstruction or observation. The alarm should be linked with either a private monitoring station or the local police department.

Panic alarms should also be installed in the offices of managers and human resource personnel who might be targeted for assault by customers or current or former employees. Conference rooms and other areas used for employee grievance hearings should also contain panic alarms. Alarms installed in these offices should be linked to the security office, a secretary's desk, or another area that is always occupied by a responsible employee. The employees in these areas must be trained on the procedures to follow when the alarm is activated. Contacting the police or the security department should be included in the procedures. (Additional information on duress alarms appears in Chapter 8.)

Safes should be provided in areas where employees exchange cash with the public. Employees should be instructed to deposit cash receipts either at designated time intervals or when a specific amount of cash is in the register. Do not give attendants the combination to the safe. In retail establishments, signs should be posted on the entrance doors stating that there is less than a given dollar amount on hand and that the attendant does not have access to the safe.

Signs and warning labels can also provide security. Signs are reasonably inexpensive and semi-permanent. Many companies 'advertise' the security measures used in their building at entrances. Warning labels such as "Premise protected by surveillance cameras" may encourage the would-be robber to search for a less secured target. Other signs can be used to direct all visitors and vendors to the main entrance. Other signs useful for preventing robberies include "No cash carried," "All cash deposited immediately into safe," and "Security Guard on duty." Most office supply stores carry "bumper sticker" paper that a company can use to design their own signs at a very reasonable rate.

Interior and exterior lighting should also be viewed as a security measure to prevent crime from occurring on or near the premise. On the inside of the building, all stairways, elevators, and any other areas that might be vulnerable for lone employees should have adequate lighting as well as an emergency backup lighting system.

The exterior areas of the building—including the entryways, receiving areas, parking areas, garages, and walkways should be well illuminated. Burned-out light bulbs should be replaced regularly. Other areas, such as shrubs and trash bins, that might provide an assailant cover should be either removed or lit enough to make hiding difficult. Security managers should routinely examine the exterior of the building to ensure security measures are in order. While it may be the job of the facility management department to change light bulbs, it will be the security manager sitting through the deposition if an assault occurs.

Security equipment should make unauthorized entry into the facility more difficult and detection of intruders easier. Security officers should respond to suspicious activities, threats, assaults, and trespassers. They should stand by on terminations, be present at layoffs, and assist in controlling picketing lines at strikes. Security managers should assist in evaluating threats. Many of the services that security officers perform are reactive rather than proactive in nature.

SECURITY MANAGEMENT

Managing a security staff is in some ways similar to managing other staffs. The security manager must deal with the typical issues of absenteeism, illness, vacations, poor performance, and the like. However, a security staff has enough unique features to make the job a challenge for even the most practiced manager. The security manager must also deal with such issues as continued security coverage over holidays and weekends. The use of force, continual and specialized training, staff retention, and boredom are also issues that the security manager must address.

A communication system that all security officers can easily use without elaborate skills must be established. Systems that may work include voice mail, email, or written notes. An integral part of any security department are the log reports that security officers should be required to fill out for every shift. Security officers should be trained to write complete and accurate reports on every incident that occurs on their shift. Shoddy reports should be rewritten until they meet acceptable standards. It's a worthy investment for the company to pay for report writing classes to improve employees skills. If you ever have to take the stand to defend a poorly written security report, you'll wish you had invested in the training.

TRAINING

A rule of thumb for every security department should be to train, train, and retrain. Security officers who lack proper training can cost a company significantly more than any training program conducted. Hiring a lawyer to defend against negligent security training can cost big bucks. When you add settlements and punitive damages, you could be looking at millions of dollars.

Before establishing a training program, it is a good idea to ask your legal counsel to advise on the areas most targeted for litigation and to specify any training required by state law. These topics should be the minimum requirements of the program. When security officers carry weapons, your company insurance carrier may be able to assist in determining training needs in addition to those imposed by state law. (See the box "Security Training Topics.")

Once you have identified the training topics, develop a training topic calendar. Classes that need to be repeated periodically should be kept on the training calendar on an annual or quarterly basis, whichever is applicable. When all your security staff is required to annually take the re-certification course on cardiopulmonary resuscitation (CPR), it's amazing how fast the year goes by. When it's in the annually published training calendar, the security officers will be less likely to claim scheduling conflicts as a reason not to attend the training.

Security Training Topics

- Blood-borne pathogens

- Bomb threats

- Building safety

- Cardiopulmonary resuscitation (CPR) and first aid

- Dealing with the public

- Handling aggressive and violent behavior

- Patrol techniques

- Report writing

- Search and seizure

- Self-defense

- Weapon retention and control

- Emergency response procedures

Security is a small piece of the overall picture when it comes to preventing workplace violence. Security personnel, practices, and equipment can do a lot to protect employees, visitors, and customers. However, security measures are much more effective when they are combined with a wide range of additional company policies and procedures that support security services.

REFERENCES

1. Mickey Veich, "Uncover the Resume Ruse," *Security Management* (October 1994): p. 75.

2. B. Filipczak, "Armed and Dangerous at Work," *Training* (July 1993): p. 42.

PART THREE
DURING WORKPLACE VIOLENCE

Intimidation and Threats

Perhaps some readers have had their life threatened by a violent act or have been threatened at some level by the actions of another human being. Indeed, most people have, at least once in their life, felt threatened with kicks, punches, retaliation, or household items flying past their head at a high velocity. For those who have felt the pain and fear of a hostile environment, I offer my empathy and support. You're not alone. For those who have not felt threatened, I sincerely hope you never do.

Intimidation is a terrible thing to feel. The victim of intimidation is often a spouse, child, parent, or coworker of a person who does not realize the extent of his or her actions.

Individuals use intimidating or threatening behavior as a means of gaining control over other people or situations. Because intimidation is a common control method that has existed since the beginning of civilization, it must in some way be effective for the abuser.

Those who use intimidation to control others may never know the true results of their actions. They fail to recognize the detrimental effect that their behavior has on those around them. Many times, though, they do know the results of their actions and are looking for a specific response in another person's behavior. The desired response might be fright, terror, panic, compliance, obedience, or submission.

Employees who feel the effects of intimidation or harassment need an immediate resolution of this situation. If the problem is not resolved, the company, the community, and the victim's family will all be added to the victim list. All will eventually suffer the consequences of this unacceptable behavior.

The victim of intimidation or harassment can use certain methods to regain control over the incident. These methods should be initiated after the first episode of intimidation or harassment. For employees, the first line of defense is to report the suspicious or violent behavior to their immediate supervisor. If the intimidation included an immediate threat, local police should be summoned without hesitation. Employees have the right to be protected from physical harm by everyone, including customers, fellow employees, managers, and family members.

Guidelines for responding to intimidation vary according to the situation. It is always better to overreact and be on the side of safety. Remember, the intimidation and threats not only affect the recipient, but every employee, customer, and bystander in the area. Customers who perceive your company as a place where intimidation is tolerated will take their business elsewhere.

Intimidation often starts with comments, looks, or other behavior that the recipient may not recognize as abusive until it becomes intolerable. The abuse may begin with verbal intimidation, cruel jokes, and negative comments and then expand to include other controlling and abuse actions. The recipient may only gradually become aware of the control that the abuser has over his or her well being. The victim may have a difficult time deciding when and where to draw the line on what is permissible.

Company policy must dictate that no form of intimidation or harassment will be tolerated at any level of the organization. The policy must state that all reported incidents of intimidation will be thoroughly investigated and that disciplinary action will be taken when needed. A sample policy statement is included in Chapter 4.

DEALING WITH AGGRESSIVE OR INTIMIDATING BEHAVIOR

Handling aggressive or intimidating behavior is definitely not on every manager's top-ten list of things he or she wants to do, but there comes a time when virtually all managers must confront a person who acts in an aggressive or intimidating manner. Often, this is a person whose behavior has been ignored for a long time. The anxiety of dealing with this person has caused the manager to postpone the inevitable.

Remember that in the overwhelming majority of cases, aggressive and hostile behavior does not result in violence. However, research does indicate that if people are trained in reacting to aggressive and intimidating behavior, they are much better able to handle situations involving aggression and their reaction time to incidents is tremendously enhanced.

Imagine the unusual scenario in which an employee has a history of verbal or physical abuse. The employee may be somebody you just don't trust. Maybe he stands 6'7", weighs 300 pounds, and his physical presence alone is intimidating. Maybe the mere thought of being alone in the same room with this person is scary.

Fear is a peculiar thing. When people talk about fear, they treat it as a negative emotion that they should not feel. Experiencing fear does not make people feel good about themselves. Some people see fear as a weakness. There is a reason we feel fear, and understanding the purpose of fear assists in handling it. Generally speaking, fear helps keep us safe. Fear is an instinct that is similar to the need for food or sleep. Feelings of fear are survival mechanisms.

Think about the reason why you don't touch a hot stove. You fear getting burned and the pain that will follow. The same is true of hundreds of activities that we either do or don't do because of the consequences. For the most part, fear should not be ignored, but nor should it consume all your actions and paralyze you. View fear as a warning signal, and use it to your advantage.

When dealing with an employee who makes you feel uncomfortable, take precautions to protect yourself and those around you. Then ensure that the encounter fulfills the objectives set forth for the meeting. Planning is a must. If the purpose of the meeting is to discuss performance related issues, follow recommended procedures for counseling or disciplining employees. Before you inform the employee of the meeting, make sure that you have taken care of all of the preliminary details.

A conference room or other private room should be reserved to guarantee privacy. Before bringing the employee into the room, make sure the room is suitable for the meeting. It should be reasonably kept and orderly. A box of facial tissue should be accessible in the event that the employee starts to cry. By having the tissue available, you eliminate the need for the employee to leave the room. Also have a plastic pitcher or glass of water available for similar reasons.

Objects that could be used as weapons should be removed from the room or put away, out of plain view. Although almost any object could be used as a weapon, the room does not have to be completely barren. Scissors, letter openers, staplers, and paperweights should not be readily accessible. Remove the temptation by removing those objects.

If you think that the employee may become hostile or aggressive, do not inform him or her of the meeting in advance. Do not allow the employee to get personal belongings to take with them to the meeting. Women should not be allowed the opportunity to get their purses.

Give some thought to the best person to conduct the meeting. If a personality conflict exists between the supervisor and the employee, a manager or another person, such as human resource staff, may be better suited to conduct or attend the meeting. This person can also serve as a witness to the events that take place in the room.

Inviting a third party to attend the meeting is a good idea when the person conducting the meeting feels intimidated by the employee. Although the third party might not have an active role on the meeting, there is strength in numbers and the moral support of the third person may be enough to keep the situation under control.

If you are worried about the possible violent reaction of the employee, notify building security, if available. A security officer's presence can be as discreet or as obvious as the situation warrants. Consider expanding company policy to require some type of security presence during particular types of meetings.

Summon uniformed officers when you want their presence to be obvious. If a softer, more discreet presence is required, use non-uniformed security officers or off-duty police officers. Officers in plain clothes may be less intimidating to the employee and offer the advantage of surprise if the situation sours.

Post the security officer within earshot just outside the room. An adjoining room may allow the security officer to hear the tone of the conversation without putting a glass to the door. An adjoining conference room also allows the security officer's presence to remain undetected.

The security officer should be trained on when and how to intervene appropriately in the meeting. Part of this decision should be up to the manager or supervisor who is conducting the meeting. His or her own comfort level must be taken into consideration, as should the employee's typical behavior. The employee may have history of becoming loud and boisterous without showing indications of violent behavior. A signal can be set up in advance to alert the security officer to enter.

The security officer can also be placed in the room during the meeting. This should only be done when a direct threat is perceived, unless company policy dictates otherwise. For some people, the presence of a security officer in the room makes them more defensive and more prone to aggressive behavior. If the security officer is stationed inside the room during the meeting, he or she should not interfere with the meeting unless necessary. The employee being disciplined or terminated might try to bring the security officer into the conversation by asking: "Do you think that's fair" or "Why are you here?" The security officer should not make comments or offer personal opinions.

Walk into the room before the employee and place a notebook or some other object in the chair closest to the door, forcing the employee to occupy another chair. This should be done as subtly as possible. An easy exit from the room is useful in case you need to leave or security personnel need to enter in a hurry. Think of the employee as a potential fire. You don't want that fire coming between you and the exit. Maintain a comfortable distance between you and the employee. If you feel intimidated by the employee, a distance of at least four to six feet is ideal.

During the conversation, remain calm and in control. The employee may intentionally try to throw you off course or to gain control of the meeting. When the employee starts giving too much direction to the conversation regain control with such comments as, "We're not here to talk about Joe." Keep the dialogue focused on the employee's performance and the actions needed to improve performance.

Pay attention to body language. You want your body to send the same message as your mouth. Use your body language to reflect control and calm. Maintain direct eye contact with the employee. Don't look around the room or at others in the room. This could give the employee the impression that you are struggling to maintain control.

When sitting at a table, keep your hands on the table or by your sides, away from your face. Do not wave your arms in the air when trying to make a point. The employee may feel threatened or possibly even challenged. You want your actions to set the example for the employee. If the employee is already excited, you don't want to magnify that level of excitement with rapid body motions. If you are using excessive emotional gestures, this signals to the employee that they may use the excessive emotional gestures too.

During the meeting, the employee may become agitated or irate. When this happens, your approach and mannerisms are especially important. The appropriate actions in this situation depend on the circumstances and your level of comfort with this individual.

It may be appropriate to continue the conversation at a later time, giving the employee the opportunity to cool down and think about matters. If you follow this course of action, tell the employee when you expect to resume the conversation. Do not set the meeting for more than a few hours or, at a maximum, a day later. Do not offer the employee this brief break if you believe that he or she might use this time to secure a weapon.

When you call a break in the meeting, do not lead the employee into believing that the matter is settled. If an employee thinks that everything has been resolved, when they are called back to continue the discussion, they might think they are being disciplined twice for the same misconduct or mistake. This will seem unfair to them—and rightfully so.

If the employee becomes irate, attempt to calm him or her down before continuing the conversation or calling a break. Be a good listener. Whether you believe that an employee is right or not, he or she still has a right to voice an opinion. Some employees are able to calm themselves down if allowed the opportunity to vent their frustrations or concerns. This does not mean they have the right to be verbally or physically abusive to others. Control must be maintained.

Allow the employee to talk about what he or she believes the problem to be and to offer a resolution. Allowing the employee to talk may bring out possible solutions. It may also uncover other problems that may be responsible for the employee's unacceptable behavior or performance. For example, perhaps the employee has been late and irritable every day for the past month because a family member is severely sick or has a terminal illness.

As the employee talks, be sensitive and empathetic to what is said. Try to understand the employee's perspective of the problem. The employee may be facing a personal problem of which you had no knowledge. Use your management and people skills to guide you through these situations. A common cliché is that people should leave their problems at home and not take them to work with them. To answer one cliché with another, this is much easier said than done. Managers and supervisors should not pretend to know the answers to the employee's problems, especially if they have never faced similar circumstances. Referral to an employee-assistance program or local not-for-profit counseling program might be the best answer. Everybody in supervisory positions should be able to quickly provide the names of community agencies that provide counseling services.

It may best serve the company to be lenient with employees when they are facing pressing personal problems that time will resolve. When the employee has a long, productive tenure with the company, the consideration you show will make this person even more dedicated after the personal problem is resolved.

The vast majority of cases involving irate employees do not end in a display of violent behavior. Do not overreact, and do not become overly paranoid.

As the employee talks, be positive and supportive. Simple nods will show the employee that he or she has your attention. Words like *yes* and *okay* are good to use to encourage a person who is upset. Do not agree with what the person is saying, however, if the statements are not statements with which you agree. Do not agree if the person says the company stinks, but instead use words to show you are listening. Talking can go a long ways towards helping a person cool down and become composed again. Use time to your advantage.

During the meeting, look for changes in behavior that indicate that the employee may be on the verge of becoming violent. The signs of potentially violent behavior are discussed in the next section.

SIGNS OF POTENTIALLY VIOLENT BEHAVIOR

Hostile customers or employees usually display warning signs that indicate that they are moving towards violence. By understanding these warning signs, you give yourself the opportunity to recognize the level of threat present and to prepare to protect yourself and others. Early recognition should allow you time to act to defuse the situation before violence erupts.

People generally act as they have acted before. The person with a history of violence against coworkers, family members, other people, or animals should be considered to have a propensity towards violence. This history should be used as a warning sign that the person is capable of behaving violently.

Agitation can display itself physically in the form of resistive tension, which is a physical response in the body that prepares a person for a fight. The blood supply to the muscles increases, for example. Chances are the person may not even be aware of this reaction. Indications of resistive attention include the clenching of fists and a general tightening of the muscles. In a sense, the person is flexing the body's muscles to warm them up.

Employees or customers may display excessive emotional attention along with exaggerated body movements. Key indicators of this are yelling, screaming, and possibly swearing. Their voices will get louder and louder; they might begin to talk with their hands, wave their arms around, pound their fists on the table, or make rude gestures. They may even kick and stomp their feet.

Employee or customers may go from this activity to a sudden cessation of all movement. They may become very quiet, almost calm, while they plan out their next move. The next move may be a renewed attempt to talk rationally and to calm themselves down. They may suddenly have realized that their conduct is inappropriate and may attempt to regain composure. However, the cessation of movement could also indicate that the person is finished discussing the matter. He or she may have decided that there is nothing you can do or say to help them and that more talk is a waste of time.

During the sudden quiet while the person is deciding on future action, maintain extreme caution. You don't know what the person is going to do next. If he or she has a history of violent behavior, you could be faced with a tough time ahead. Consider whether to summon security or other backup personnel to the scene. If a panic button is available, this might be the time to use it. Because every situation is different, it is impossible to predict what actions are optimal at all times.

Immediately before a person becomes violent, he or she may display one or more of the following actions. When these signs are present, presume the person is ready to become violent. Control the distance between you and the other person. Be prepared to use a bailout route.

The person may take on what is referred to as a *boxer stance*. The legs of the person will be shoulder-width apart, and one leg will be slightly ahead of the other in a balanced position. The person may start clenching their hands or positioning them in an offensive manner. The shoulders may shift back and forth as if the person were trying to stretch them out. This is sometimes called the *shoulder-shrug*.

The person may quickly search the area behind you, looking for others that might come to your defense. People who are prone to fight are usually less willing to engage in a physical encounter if they know that others will be quick to respond.

As with the any warning signs, at the first sign of violence, immediately notify the local police and building security, if available. (See the box "Assessing Signs of Potentially Violent Behavior.")

Assessing Signs of Potentially Violent Behavior

- People who have been violent before may have a propensity towards violence.

- Agitation can display itself in the form of resistive tension.

- Many people clench their hands into fists, do shoulder shrugs, or get into a "boxer stance" before a physical confrontation.

- The person may yell and scream, wave their hands in the air or act in a similar manner.

- The person may switch from loud behavior to total cessation of all movements.

- The person may look over your shoulders to see who else is present or may come to your defense.

- The person may tell you directly what they are planning to do (e.g., "I'm going to knock your block off").

- Security officers should be called if you expect the person might become violent.

- At the first sign of violence, call local law enforcement officials.

CHAPTER EIGHT
VIOLENT BEHAVIOR

Cathy's Story

Cathy was born and raised in the peaceful Midwest where, even though crime existed, it never significantly touched her life. In her early thirties, she was happily married to a serviceman and had young children. Like other wives of servicemen, Cathy packed up the family periodically and followed her husband from base to base. She worked outside the home, leaving her children at childcare.

In other words, Cathy was a lot like of other working women in the United States. On June 20, 1994, that changed. Cathy now has a story to tell that the rest of us never want to experience. She was the victim of workplace violence. She survived, but many others did not.

During our interview, Cathy's qualities were quick to surface. She is emotionally strong, intelligent, brave, and is surrounded by the love of family and friends. Cathy made it through the ordeal without severe emotional injuries. She was in many ways, very lucky.

I'm relaying Cathy's story in the hope that others will realize the traumatic effects that violence can produce and will take whatever steps are necessary to prevent violence. Violence can and does happen in every neighborhood, including the one in which you work and live.

Cathy moved to the Spokane, Washington, area in the beginning of 1993. After settling in, she took a civilian job as a medical clerk in a mental health clinic located in the annex of the Fairchild Air Force Base Hospital. Cathy had worked there for about a year when tragedy struck. A former patient, Dean Mellberg, returned to the clinic and killed five people and wounded twenty-three others.

During the year that Cathy worked at the clinic before the incident, she scheduled appointments, filed paperwork, took dictation, and performed other clerical tasks. She never received any formal training on dealing with violent or hostile behavior. Looking back, she was never aware of any emergency plans for dealing with violence, but she was sure that the hospital had them. She thought the emergency room staff had probably been through training, as that was probably the site of the greatest danger.

The office where Cathy worked was across the parking lot from the main hospital. She worked on the first floor, where several doctors had offices. On June 20, just after 3:00, Cathy sat at her desk, working on her computer.

The office was empty except for one other worker. The last appointment for the day was at three, and that patient was with the doctor. Cathy heard a loud bang and, for a brief second, thought it may have been a door slamming. Then she knew it wasn't the door. Cathy knew it was gunfire coming from the room next door, Dr. London's office.

Cathy ran around the office looking for a place to hide. She describes that moment as "running around the room like a chicken with its head cut off." There were two doors leading out of the office, but both of them led to the hallway where Dr. London's and Dr. Brigham's offices were located. Not knowing the location of the assailant, she decided to stay in the reception area.

Cathy's coworker slammed and locked the door when the gunman attempted to enter the office. The coworker broke through the screen on the window and jumped out of the room. Cathy hid under her desk, pulling her feet up so they couldn't be seen. She pulled her chair in behind her to make it appear that nobody could be under the desk. As she hid, the gunman walked by.

As Cathy hid under her desk, she thought of her husband raising their children alone. She wondered how he could raise them without her. She thought of her children growing up without a mother. She heard more shots coming from the other office. She thought the shots came from Dr. Brigham's office, which was outside the other door of the office where Cathy was hiding.

Cathy knew that some employees had gathered outside the building to smoke. She heard a woman pleading with the gunman not to shoot her, and then Cathy heard more shots. Cathy, while still hiding under the desk, wondered how many of the six women gathered there were killed.

An unidentified man frantically announced over the public address (PA) system that a gunman was loose in the building and that everybody should leave the hospital. Then he announced that the gunman was outside and that everybody should get back inside. Cathy knew by the shots fired at the pleading woman that the gunman was outside.

Cathy got to a telephone and called her husband. She told him that a gunman was loose in the building, killing people, and then she said she had to go. She went back to hiding under her desk. She had no idea how many gunmen there were or why they were there. She thought they were terrorists, possibly from another country.

Chaos filled the offices. Cathy could hear people screaming, gunshots, and sirens. She didn't know if the police were firing back or if all the shot were coming from the assailant. More frantic announcements came over the PA system. A "code blue" was called for the doctors that had been shot.

A man entered the lobby. For a moment, Cathy didn't know if he was the gunman or somebody else. He was bleeding from a gunshot to his leg. When he said something like, "What is he doing?" Cathy knew that the man was not the assailant. Cathy wanted to help stop the man's bleeding. She tried to remember where the latex gloves were and then realized that they did not have any in the office. She hid under the desk again, and the bleeding man hid under another desk.

A group of people broke into the office. They were medics and military police. They ordered everybody outside. Cathy went to Dr. Brigham's office and saw him on the floor. Even though the medics were all around him, she could tell that he was dead. Dr. London's patient was still in the office. Cathy took the patient and did what she was told to do—run. She and many others ran down the street, into the military housing area located off the base.

In the housing area, people were mowing their lawns and children were playing outside. They hadn't a clue as to what was happening. Cathy yelled for everybody to get inside their houses.

Cathy was let into a nearby house to hide with perhaps four other people. From this house, Cathy called her parents and told them what was going on. The call was very short because nobody knew where the gunman was and they had to hide.

Cathy recalls how strange it was to hear somebody knock on the door of the house. She remembers wondering whether somebody should answer the door. What if it was the gunman? Somebody did answer the door, and there were military police outside the house. The people hiding in the house were told to evacuate because the gunman was loose.

Again the people in the house began running down the street, toward the military base. Cathy remembers thinking that being in the street wasn't safe because they didn't know where the gunman was, but she ran anyway. She ran until she got outside the fence at the base. Then she stopped. People, lots of people, were there. They stood around not knowing what to do next.

Sirens filled the air, and they seemed to be coming from everywhere. Reporters with cameras were already there, and more were arriving. The reporters had to stay on the other side of the fence, away from the people who ran to the base.

Cathy's husband found her at the base, and after a while they were allowed to leave. Cathy did not go directly home; first she stopped at the home of a coworker. From conversations with coworkers and others at the base, she found out that Dr. Brigham and Dr. London were both dead.

The next three days were filled with telephone calls from family and friends. Cathy's parents, who had left Spokane just days earlier, comforted and consoled her over the telephone. She told her story over and over. Everybody wanted to know all of the details. It wasn't until the day after the shootings that Cathy found out who the gunman was. She immediately recognized his name from the news reports. He was a former patient whom the doctors had recommended be discharged.

Cathy felt tremendous exhaustion in the days that followed. She attended a memorial service for those who were killed on June 20. Even though she felt as if the doctors were members of her family, she did not attend either funeral because she wasn't sure she would make it through the services. Only a week earlier they had all gone on a picnic together. Cathy's loss was tremendous.

Grief counselors were brought in for all employees, even those who were not there on the day of the shooting. At first, Cathy didn't want to go to the mandatory counseling sessions. After it was all over, she was glad that she had. The friends and coworkers who were affected by the slayings banded together after the incident to form their own informal support group. They talked among themselves, consoled one another, and helped one another recover from the incident.

During the week that followed the shooting, the slightest noise in the night woke Cathy. She jumped out of bed and hid on the floor, afraid of the gunfire that she was sure had followed her.

Within days of the shooting, tragedy struck again. An air force plane crashed, killing the four people aboard. Cathy was sitting at home on the afternoon of the crash. The sounds of the sirens again filled the air. Not knowing what had happened, Cathy went outside and saw smoke everywhere. Neighbors also went into their yards and into the streets. A neighbor had said that a plane had crashed. The second trauma only compounded the first.

A week later, Cathy returned to the office for the first time. She was terrified by the thought of entering the building where she had hidden under the desk to escape the gunman's bullets. When she entered the lobby she saw, felt, and smelled a place different than what she had left.

The furniture was in disarray, moved out of the way and stacked on other pieces of furniture. The old blood-soaked carpet had been ripped out and replaced. The walls were in the process of being repainted. The doctors' offices had been stripped. Repair crews were still working to clean up the mess the assailant had left behind.

With the office in such disarray, there was very little work that Cathy could do. Patients were not seen. Every now and then she would have to pull a file for somebody, but for the most part, she stood around and talked to people who came by to pay their respects. Cathy felt frustrated at the fact that there was no work to do. She wondered why she was there. She felt employees should not have to go back until they were ready for them to work. The next day she stayed home.

Cathy and her husband decided to leave the area after the plane crash. The requested a humanitarian transfer, which was later granted. Cathy again packed up the family and followed her husband to a different base. The new base was within driving distance of her family.

This time, the move was different. The trauma she endured with friends and coworkers resulted in a unique bond between them. They had cared for and helped one another during a very difficult time. In some ways, Cathy felt like she was abandoning people she cared about. She was escaping the building and the base that served as a daily reminder of the events that happened on June 20.

When asked how the tragedy changed her, Cathy says that she now has a greater appreciation for the meaning of life. For now, she no longer works outside the home. Instead she treasures the time she can spend with her children. Cathy is much more safety conscious than ever before. She doesn't trust other people the way she once did. She's more aware of her surroundings and the people around her and her children. For Cathy, the lesson learned from the shooting is that people should trust their instincts. When you sense that somebody or something is not safe, trust your feelings.

Cathy feels lucky to have survived the incident without permanent emotional damage. She believes that because she was emotionally healthy before the incident, received counseling afterward, and, most important, had friends and family to provide support, she has been able to leave the trauma behind her without too much difficulty.

FIGHT OR FLIGHT

When violence erupts on the workplace, seconds count. When robbery is the cause of the violence, follow the recommended procedures in the next section for surviving a robbery. When the violence is caused by an estranged spouse, a current or former employee, or somebody else, you need to protect yourself and as many other people as possible.

This is not the time to play hero. Most heroes are dead. This is the time to remain calm and to think rationally. If you are the target of the violence, do what the assailant says if doing so will protect your safety.

Do try to escape if you can do so safely. If you are in the room with the assailant and are near an open doorway, you may try to escape if another person distracts the assailant. Do not be obvious. Be as quiet as possible. You do not want to bring attention to yourself or to your movements. If you are able to get out of the room, go to the safest place possible. Lock the doors, close the blinds or shades and call the police. Thinking clearly in an emergency can be extremely difficult, but do try to stay as rational as possible. You may be the only person with the opportunity to call the police and summon help. Your coworkers and customers may be depending on you.

When you are in a room away from the assailant, keep your presence secret. Do what you can to block the assailant from coming into the room. Again, lock the doors and close the blinds if possible. If the room has a separate exit to the exterior of the building or away from the main center of violence, go. Gain as much distance as you can and try to get into a protected area as quickly as possible. Do not maintain a straight line of vision with the assailant, you want to stay as hidden as possible. If you work in an office with many hallways and cubicles, turn down different hallways as soon you make your way to an exit or secure room. Call the police as soon as you can do so safely.

Do not try to confront the individual unless that is your only option. At a seminar dealing with workplace security and violence, an older woman in the audience asked what to do if confronted by a person with a gun or a knife. I was shocked when the speaker advised participants to grab the weapon from the assailant's hands. The room erupted with a barrage of questions: How could a sixty-five year old woman without personal defense training disarm a young man with a semi-automatic rifle? How could somebody safely take a knife away from a crazed person on drugs? How could an untrained person take a gun away from an assailant who doesn't want to give it up?

The truth is, they typically can't. There are occasional stories about a receptionist who outwits a robber, but these stories are few and far between. Just as a person trained in first aid should not attempt to perform heart bypass surgery, a person untrained in countermeasures should not attempt to disarm a person with a weapon. In most cases, the attempt would be suicidal. Even for people who have training in this type of tactical maneuver, it should be a last resort. Ideally, once you give assailants what they want, they will leave. Only in a true life-or-death situation should you attempt heroic measures.

In some cases, trying to overpower the assailant is your only hope for survival or the survival of someone else for whom you are willing to give up your life. If you know that by doing nothing you will be killed, you don't have much to lose by attempting to escape or fight. Run away if you can; fight only as a last resort. Between 1993 and 1999, of the 12,328,000 acts of violence, only 2.7 percent of the victims physically resisted the assailant.[1]

Scott's Story

According to the U.S. Department of Labor's 1993 Census of Fatal Occupational Injuries, 1,063 people were murdered on the job in 1993. The vast majority of those killed (75 percent) were murdered during a robbery. This is the story of one of those victims, Scott Meyer. His parents, Norbert and Martha, tell Scott's story. The Meyers' only child was murdered at eight o'clock in the evening on October 12, 1993, during a robbery at the convenience store where he worked.

To understand the tragedy of Scott's murder, we must understand his parents. Norbert is successfully self-employed in contract construction. He has spent his entire life earning an honest living to support his family. He is a large man with a loud but gentle voice that quivers when he talks about his son. Although he says that he does not mind talking about his son's murder, when given the opportunity, he'll change the subject. Right now, there's only one other matter that he talks about with intensity; reinstating the death penalty in the state where his son was murdered.

Scott's mother, Martha, is a woman whom almost any child would be happy to call mom. She looks like the stereotypical grandmother who bakes cookies and does crafts in her spare time. She's retired from a job at the local hospital where she had worked for many years. Martha is an intelligent woman who takes obvious pride in her home and family. Despite her grandmotherly appearance, she does not, and never will, have grandchildren. Instead, she finds company with her pet terrier.

The Meyers had thought about giving the terrier away to friends three months before Scott's death, but Scott convinced his parents to keep the dog. Martha believes that Scott's determination to keep the dog is now almost ironic because after Scott's death, the terrier played an important role in Martha's recovery.

Inside their historic, two-story house, pictures of Scott are a silent reminder of the son they lost. A yellowed copy of their son's obituary hangs on the side of the refrigerator. Artwork created by Scott in his younger days is displayed with pride in the living room. A painting of an American flag and an eagle that hangs over the fireplace, was a father-son project many years ago. The painting is a testimony to the family's belief in patriotism and freedom.

The Meyers describe their son as a responsible adult who was independent at the time of his death, yet lived at home with them. He led a quiet and private life. Scott never married and considered himself a "confirmed bachelor." He enjoyed activities with his parents as well as time spent with his friends.

Scott had worked at the same convenience store for seventeen of his thirty-four years. He worked at other second jobs during his life, but he especially enjoyed working at the convenience store. The manager of the store and Scott had been close friends for a number of years, and they enjoyed a good working relationship. Scott also enjoyed talking with customers, many of whom he knew by name and had gone to school with.

Having been robbed twice before, Scott knew about the potential for violent crime at convenient stores. A year earlier, the manager had been shot during a robbery. The bullet grazed the top of his head but did not injure him seriously.

Scott's father described the convenience store as "just a violent place." Over the years Scott's parents tried to convince him to quit his job and find safer work. Scott typically replied that he wasn't afraid of the customers and that he enjoyed his job. According to his mother, his feelings may have started to change in the weeks before his death. On September 29, two weeks before Scott's murder, a local man was murdered on the job at a laundry. No arrest was ever made in the case. Scott's parents believe that it could have been the same men who murdered their son, but there was not enough evidence for an arrest.

After the murder at the laundry, Scott repeatedly told his friends and parents that he didn't believe he would ever see his thirty-fifth birthday and that perhaps it was time to move to another town. Scott's mother tried again to convince him to find safer employment. Instead, he reluctantly agreed to visit an attorney to have his will drawn up. He never did.

The Meyers describe the security in the store as almost nonexistent. The store had two entrances: one facing the street and one in the back of the store. Because the gas pumps were located on both sides of the store, the back door was locked only after nine in the evening. The store had no security cameras. Scott never mentioned to his parents receiving formal training on robbery prevention or what to do if a robbery occurred. In an interview with the press, the public relations director told reporters that employees are trained in robbery prevention and that a list of robbery prevention and survival tips was posted on the bathroom walls at all stores. The store had a floor safe, and company policy stated that whenever the attendant had $100 in cash he or she was to drop the money in the safe. The store also had a policy that employees were not allowed to bring weapons into the store. A robbery alarm was located near the cash register.

A local county supervisor visited the store almost nightly to socialize with Scott and the other clerks. Store security was a topic of discussion every night. The county supervisor was appalled by the lack of security provided for the employees. He described the store as a "violent tragedy waiting to happen." According to the county supervisor, after the sun went down, customers frequented the store with guns sticking out of their belts and pockets, and it was "a scary place to be." Because he knew that employees were barred from bringing guns to work with them, he brought his own gun with him. After the murder the county supervisor posted $1,000 of his own money as a reward for leading to the arrest and conviction of the murderers.

A month before his death, Scott asked the local supervisor to help him find a different job. Scott wanted to leave the convenience store where he had invested so many years of his life because of the constant threat of violence.

On the day that he was murdered, Scott went to work as he had always done. Meanwhile, ex-convict Keith Taylor and another man, Reginald Nelson, roamed the city. The police wanted Taylor for questioning in another murder in Saginaw, Michigan. A few miles away from the store the two men kidnapped a woman who was parking her van in front of her house. They forced her into the back of the van and drove off with her. The kidnappers never injured her; apparently they just wanted transportation to use during the upcoming robbery.

After driving around for a few minutes, the two men drove up to the back of the convenience store and entered through the back door. The evidence that remained can only piece together what happened in the store. Moments after they entered the store, the woman in the back of the van heard a gunshot. She knew immediately that the men had shot the store attendant. Court records indicate that Meyer had been beaten before being shot in the head with a .357 Magnum. Medical experts believe he died instantly.

The robbers left the store and got back into the van and started to drive. The woman felt certain that she, too, would be shot. After driving around, the men pulled into a parking lot at an apartment building only a few blocks away. They got out of the van, leaving the woman in the back with the keys in the ignition. They told her to count to 100, and they fled. Moments later, when the men had not returned, the woman jumped onto the driver's seat and sped away.

The Meyers were sitting at home that evening at 9:15 when the store manager's wife and a police officer knocked on the door. The manager's wife told the Meyers that their son was dead. Moments later, Scott's best friend, Jeff, arrived. Jeff had heard on the radio that a male employee had been shot at the store. He immediately knew that it had been Scott.

Jeff and Norbert Meyer drove to the store as friends and neighbors began arriving at the house. Norbert parked his truck in the parking lot and watched the police tape off the area and begin their work. He didn't need to go into the store. The manager's wife had already identified the body.

The murder occurred on Tuesday and the two men were arrested on Thursday. The man later identified as the gunman, Reginald Nelson, was nineteen years old. The other man, Taylor, was twenty-six and had already served seven years on a previous robbery conviction. Nelson was convicted of kidnapping, robbery, and murder. He is serving a life sentence without the possibility of parole. Taylor is serving a sentence of forty-five to sixty years.

These days, Scott's parents are advocates of the death penalty. Norbert led a statewide campaign for the reinstatement of the death penalty. The Meyers also favor legislation mandating security equipment and training for businesses that deal with cash and are open to the public late at night.

During the robbery, the sum of $73 was taken.

KEY ELEMENTS OF A ROBBERY

Before planning the actions to be taken after a robbery, it is important to understand the key elements of this type of crime. Employee education on the facts about robbery will displace misconceptions regarding this crime and will help employees act in a manner that does not put them or others in additional danger. Educate employees about the following:

* The fallacy of the "typical robber" stereotype

- Techniques and methods used by criminals in planning a robbery

- The robber's conduct during the crime

There is no such thing as a typical robber, and it is dangerous to assume that there is. Employees who expect a robber to fit a television stereotype are vulnerable to robbers who don't match their preconceived image. There are recorded cases of robbers ranging in age from eight to seventy-nine years old. There have been female robbers who committed robberies while carrying an infant or small child. A robber can be any age, race, or gender.

The myths commonly associated with bank robberies include the following:

- Two or more bandits hold all employees and customers at gunpoint. This is probably the most common scenario played out in the movies. (Remember *Bonnie and Clyde*?)

- A lone bandit stands out from the business' customers by dress or appearance. The out-of-place bandit is easily identified the moment he walks into the building, allowing the attendant plenty of time to activate the duress alarm.

The truth is that fewer than 20 percent of all robberies are of the mass holdup type, and it is usually impossible to identify robbers by their dress or appearance. The robber may be dressed in blue jeans and a sweatshirt or a suit and tie. He or she is usually not looking to attract attention.

During the late eighties and early nineties, there was an increase in a certain type of robber in Florida and California: the "crack robber." Crack robbers wear sunglasses and a baseball cap to hide their faces from the security cameras. Many legitimate customers often dress in the same manner.

In the United States, the highest percentage of occupational homicides result from robberies. Convenience stores, liquor stores, hotels, and motels are a few of the businesses that are the most susceptible to robbery. In 1993, it was estimated that in the U.S. $538 million was lost in 659,757 reported robberies. There were over 50,000 robberies in 1993 in convenience stores, gas stations, and service stations. The average dollar loss in a convenience store robbery was $449. In the same year there were nearly 12,000 bank robberies with an average loss of $3,308.[2]

More typical is the late-night robbery by a sole bandit of a retail establishment. The bandit will often look for the business that offers the least amount of risk—an establishment that has a lone attendant, cash, and a limited number of customers or visibility from the street. Planning for the crime is typically minimal. The robber determines the easiest target with the most money and then waits for an opportunity to present itself. Sixty-two percent of all people arrested for robbery were under 25 years of age.[3] In many of these cases, less than $50 dollars was taken.

Most people find it difficult to imagine risking their freedom for $50. To understand the high occurrence of robberies, we must understand the robber's perspective. To the robber, that $50 probably seems like all the money in the world; the robber believes that he or she needs that $50 much more than the store does. The robber might be looking for the money to buy drugs or another bottle of booze.

More important than monetary loss, however, is the potential physical or psychological injury to the employees and customers. A business' paramount concern during a robbery should be the safety of all employees and customers.

On November 26, 2002, former employee John Taylor was sentenced to death after the brutal massacre at a Wendy's restaurant in Queens, New York. Taylor and his accomplice Craig Godineaux, a mentally retarded 32-year-old man, entered the restaurant to rob the place. After talking with the manager for a few minutes, all the employees were taken to the freezer and gagged with duct tape. Taylor allegedly shot two employees and ordered Godineaux to shoot the rest. Five employees were brutally killed and two others were shot. Godineaux received a life sentence. He was not eligible for the death sentence due to his mental retardation.

What happens during a robbery? The average robbery lasts less than sixty seconds. In appearance, the robber often looks like any other customer. The robber will single out one employee and will not try to gain the attention of other employees or customers. The robber may make demands either verbally or in writing. The robber usually demands all the money in the cash drawer and may instruct the attendant not to use "bait money," or money that activates an alarm when removed from the cash register. The robbery will involve the threat of violence—a weapon was displayed in over 60% of the robberies in 1993. Guns were displayed in 42.4% of the robberies, knives or other cutting instruments were used in 10%, and other weapons were used in 9.5%.[4] Between

1993 and 1999, a weapon of some type was used in 20.7% of all acts of workplace violence with the majority of cases falling into the Transportation (31.7%) and Retail Sales (23.3%) fields.[5]

ROBBERY DETERRENCE

Most bandits want to rob a single person and leave without attracting unnecessary attention. Their goal is to commit the crime, escape, and not be arrested. To accomplish this goal, the robber uses various criteria to select the target of the robbery. One of the physical elements that can encourage robberies is the layout of the lobby or cashier area. Minimum protection for employees and limited observation from the outside of the building works in the bandit's favor. The number and location of escape routes can aid the robber in fleeing the building and the area. Robbers usually leave the building in an unhurried manner to avoid attracting the attention of other employees or customers.

Cashiers and receptionists who fail to pay attention to activities in their areas invite robbery attempts. Clerks who do not make direct eye contact with customers are also inviting to the criminal.

To deter a robbery, employees should be aware of the total environment. A cashier who projects an image of alertness will help create an environment that is not favorable to the robber. Visible alertness is an effective deterrent to robbery.

Employees should greet each customer as he or she enters the lobby or building. Besides being an advantage for customer relations, this behavior helps deter robbers, who usually do not want to be seen before making their demands. Once the demand is made, the victim experiences fear and terror. These feelings, which are natural, prevent the victim from memorizing the robber's appearance. Instead, the victim concentrates on the robber's demands. Robbers know this and use it to their advantage. If the clerk or receptionist greets all customers and looks directly at them, he or she will be better able to identify the criminal later if a crime does occur. Direct eye contact may be all that is needed to convince the robber to take his business elsewhere.

Receptionists should be trained to recall descriptions of customers. They should look for such factors such as height and weight; hair, eye, and skin color; presence of tattoos or other distinguishing marks; clothing; and vehicles. After a little practice, they will begin to make mental notes of each customer's appearance.

Windows near the entrance where receptionists are located must be as clear as possible of all material that blocks visibility from the outside. Obscured windows offer robbers the protection of not being seen from outside the building. This reduces the robber's chances of being seen by witnesses.

Many office posters and announcements seem to find their way to the front door. Employees who put them there are not trained or educated in theft prevention. When you observe posters, birth announcements, or other materials that block visibility on doors, contact the person who displayed them. Explain why the posters should not block the view from the outside and ask that they move the materials to another location. Most employees will gladly comply with this request when they know the reasons behind it.

SURVIVING A ROBBERY

Law enforcement officials recommend various procedures to decrease the risk of harm during a robbery and to increase the chances of apprehending and convicting the robber. Instruct the employee to follow these ten guidelines during and after a robbery:

1. Avoid actions during a robbery that might increase the danger to you, other employees, or customers.

2. Activate the duress alarm system during a robbery only if you can do so safely.

3. Make a mental note of the robber's physical appearance.

4. Give the robber no more money than demanded.

5. Protect all evidence after the robbery.

6. Observe the method of escape if you can do it safely.

7. Notify local police after the robbery if they have not already arrived.

8. Control access into and out of the building.

9. Write down a list of all witnesses to the robbery.

10. Collect information concerning the robber's description and method of escape.

RESPONSIBILITIES DURING A ROBBERY

During a robbery, all employees should do the following:

- Remain calm. This may be very difficult to do, but remember that if you panic, the robber may panic also. Your reasoned actions are needed to help protect your coworkers and customers.

- Cooperate. Listen and do exactly as you are told.

- Be courteous and polite.

- Don't try to talk the robber out of the robbery. The robber decided to commit the crime before he or she entered the premises.

- Follow all instructions given. Do not argue with the robber.

- Tell the robber of any possible surprises. If you are expecting somebody to walk in for an appointment, let the robber know in advance.

- Minimize movement; do not draw attention to yourself by making quick actions. The robber could mistake these movements for defensive actions and retaliate.

- Ask permission before taking any actions. Inform the robber in advance of your actions. For example, say, "I am opening the drawer now," or, "I'm getting my keys out of my pocket." Quick, unannounced actions could startle the robber and could lead to injury.

- When possible, keep any notes that the robber gives you. They may help the police apprehend the robber and will also act as evidence later.

- Do not attempt to activate the duress alarm if it cannot be done without attracting the attention of the robber.

- Give the robber time to leave.

- Do not chase the robber after he or she has left the premises. Observe the escape route and obtain a vehicle description and license plate number only if you can do so from inside the building.

RESPONSIBILITIES AFTER A ROBBERY

The moments following a robbery are filled with emotion and chaos. However, this is the time when direct and decisive actions are needed to regain control and activate post-robbery procedures. The actions taken in the first few minutes following a robbery can assist police officers with their investigation and may lead to the arrest and prosecution of the robber(s).

Post-robbery responsibilities are divided into different categories: employee responsibilities, management responsibilities, and special assignments. The appointment of special assignment responsibilities should be determined before a robbery occurs to facilitate completion and reduce confusion.

After a robbery, all employees have the following responsibilities:

- Do not discuss the holdup with others.

- Do not touch anything in the area of the robbery.

- Trigger the duress alarm if not already done.

- When possible, without leaving the building, observe the robber's escape route and get a vehicle description and license plate number.

- Complete a physical description form.

- Be prepared to give a signed statement to police officers.

- Do not talk to the media.

- List the names and addresses of all the people who witnessed the robbery.

Management personnel have the following responsibilities:

- Remain calm as a role model for other employees.

- Escort any victims to a quiet room.

- Alert other employees of the situation.

- Ensure that the police are notified. Provide the following information:

    The building name and location

    Your name and title

    The time of the robbery

    A brief description of the robber and escape method

    Details of any injuries and whether an ambulance is needed or not

- Refer all press inquires to the designated individual.

- Notify the Employee-Assistance Program, the Security Division, and the Human Resources Division as needed.

Special Assignment 1

- Secure the reception or lobby area where the robbery took place. Block access to all areas that the robber entered, including the entrance, the rest rooms, counters, couches in the waiting area, and magazine racks.

- Protect any physical evidence.

- Pass out physical description forms and pens to all employees and customers present during the holdup. Collect the forms as they are completed, ensuring that each form has the name and the contact information of the employee or customer written legibly on it. Initial each form as it is collected. Give all completed forms to the police.

Special Assignment 2

- Lock all exterior doors.

- Station an employee at each entrance to direct emergency response personnel to the area, allow only authorized personnel to enter, discourage employees and customers from leaving. If a customer insists on leaving, obtain his or her phone number and address.

- Report any unusual situations to the police.

DURESS ALARMS

Robbers sometimes become agitated when they think an employee has activated a duress alarm. For this reason, employees should not activate the alarm unless they can do so without attracting the robber's attention.

All employees who work near a duress alarm must be instructed on its exact location. It is not sufficient to point casually to the location of the alarm. If the location of the button requires employees to bend down or get on their knees to see it, then ask them to do so. Do not let employees actually activate the alarm unless a test alarm has been set up with the local police department or monitoring unit.

Employees must also be instructed on how the system works. Inform the employees that the alarm is silent. They should not expect to hear or see anything when the alarm is activated. When they press the button they should feel reasonably assured that the alarm has been activated, and they should not panic. Employees should be told where the enunciator panel is located and who responds to the alarm. Is it security staff or the police department?

Accidental Activation of the Duress Alarm

When an alarm has been accidentally activated, it is necessary to ensure that the proper officials are notified and that the alarm is reset. An employee who knows that he or she accidentally activated the alarm must immediately contact the designated person. If the false alarm occurs during the second or third shift, the supervisor or manager should be contacted immediately.

When notified of a false alarm, call the police department and/or the monitoring station immediately to advise them that the alarm was an accident. Give them your name and title and the location of your business. A password or authorization code may be required. Remember that, unless you tell them, the police department will not know that the alarm was accidentally activated and will respond as if an actual emergency was taking place. When the police respond to a duress alarm, they usually drive at high speeds. This response is necessary during an actual emergency, but when it is a false alarm it can present an unnecessary danger to police and to civilians.

When a single location experiences several false alarms, police response typically diminishes due to the belief that all of the alarms at that location are false. This can be extremely dangerous to employees, customers, and emergency personnel responding to the alarm. Some jurisdictions fine heavily for numerous false alarms as a notice for the businesses to use their alarms in a prudent manner.

If a central monitoring station services the business, contact the agency to tell them that the alarm was false. Be prepared to give your account number or other information. The monitoring company will contact the responding police department. By having the procedures written in down in advance, the process will be accomplished in a smooth manner.

As mentioned in the foreword of this book, two women, Janice Schneider and Dawniell Beauregard, were killed during a retail robbery on October 29, 2002. If was later found that the shooter in the robbery was also a former employee. This is just one example of people being killed during a robbery in the United States, which happens on almost a daily basis. Scott Meyer's parents still anguish over the murder of their son. The importance of having effective robbery deterrence training and effective policies and procedures cannot be stressed enough.

RERERENCES

1. Bureau of Justice Statistics, Special Report. *Violence in the Workplace 1993-99.* (Washington D.C.: U.S. Government Printing Office, December 2001), p. 6.

2. U.S Department of Justice, Uniform Crime Reports: Crime in the United States (Washington, D.C.: U.S. Government Printing Office, 4 November 1994), p. 27.

3. Ibid., p. 29.

4. Ibid., p. 28.

5. Bureau of Justice Statistics, Special Report. *Violence in the Workplace 1993-99.* (Washington D.C.: U.S. Government Printing Office, December 2001), p. 7.

PART FOUR
AFTER WORKPLACE VIOLENCE HAS OCCURRED

POST-INCIDENT PLANNING

Recovery strategies should be in place before a violent event takes place. When a post-incident plan is in place, detailed instructions will be readily available to employees and will allow for quick actions and decisions. During periods of high stress, such as those following any type of disaster, it's difficult to think through and make rational decisions. Thousands of details must be dealt with and hundreds of decisions must be made.

When the decisions are made in advance and documented on paper, the recovery process is quicker and less painful for everybody involved. These prepared decisions sometimes prevent human anguish, and they sometimes save the company money and time.

The post-incident recovery plan does need not to be extremely elaborate. Procedures and policies should be decided on and written in advance. When determining recovery strategies, weigh the risk versus the cost. Recovery plans should include established time frames to expedite restoration. Vendor contracts and agreements should be included in the recovery plan, and vendor names and telephone numbers, including home telephone numbers, should be recorded. This will ease the burden later when you need to contact them in a hurry.

In some cases, telephone lines and customer service inquiries must be transferred to another location until the business is ready to reopen. Other office locations may have to cover pending manufacturing orders, if possible. It is important to maintain customer confidence during difficult times. Once customers start shopping elsewhere, it can be very difficult to regain their business.

After a violent incident, you will need to address security concerns immediately. Employees may no longer feel safe in their work environment, and they may want security controls to be tightened to almost penitentiary standards. It is not uncommon for employees to request metal detectors at every door, armed security officers, and bulletproof glass in cashier or reception areas. Management must weigh the costs versus the benefits of such long-term security measures. Employees may find the new security measures great right after an incident of workplace violence, but dislike them six months down the road after all the expenses have been paid to implement them. The presence of additional security officers within the facility will help employees feel safe as they return to work.

It is important to plan for the physical cleanup of your facility before any emergency incidents. Imagine that a company experiences a fire with moderate smoke and water damage during the night. No matter what else happens, or how much it costs, the building must be open for business at eight o'clock in the morning or the company will lose millions of dollars. Now imagine trying to negotiate a contract for the cleanup of smoke and damage at three o'clock in the morning. The company's bargaining position is nonexistent, and the cleaning company knows this. The business will get out the big checkbook for this one. The business will pay exorbitant sums to the first cleaning company that agrees to roll out of bed, if the business is lucky enough to find one!

Now imagine trying to convince a cleaning company to come in and clean up after a shooting incident involving injured employees. In Cathy's case, described in Chapter 8, bullet holes, blood, broken furniture, glass, and other debris were everywhere. Companies that have not prepared in advance for cleanup had better get the big checkbook out if they are looking at vendor services not already under contract.

Recovery from violence will be unlike recovery from fire or natural disasters. The employees, customers and the community will need to recuperate from the trauma. They may also need to grieve for the loss of friends, family members, or coworkers. Asking employees to participate in the cleanup after a violent incident is asking way too much from the employees and may hinder their personal recovery.

Business Recovery Planning

- For optimal results, recovery planning must occur before the incident.

- Once a violent incident occurs, it's too late to plan.

- Business recovery planning will lessen the impact on the business, employees, and the community.

- Employees themselves will need time to recover from the trauma of the incident, and some will be unable to participate in the recovery process.

- Business recovery planning need not be extremely elaborate.

- Preestablished agreements with vendors should be included in the plans.

- The recovery plan should include telephone numbers of all employees, names and numbers of employees' family members, and vendor names and numbers.

- All personnel who are responsible for carrying out the recovery plan should have a copy of it. Copies should also be kept off-site.

- Designate backups for key personnel.

MEDIA COVERAGE

When a violent crime is committed, you can be certain that media people will show up. The media may be on the scene before all of the emergency response people arrive. Most newspapers and television stations have an employee designated to monitor police and fire radio channels. This notifies them of the incidents almost as quickly as the local police and rescue teams. Many news agencies also have toll-free numbers for citizens who know of worthy news stories to call in and report the story. Plan on prompt arrival of reporters and television crews.

During the first few moments following a bombing, shooting, hostage taking, or robbery things will be chaotic. Not only must you ensure the safety of employees, obtain medical care for the injured, notify family members of the incident, and help police apprehend the assailant, you must also deal with the countless questions from the media. Chances are they will be asking questions that you can't answer yet. Even if you want to provide the details, you just don't know all of the facts immediately after the incident.

Media is a business just like most other businesses. Media representatives are there to do their job. Like many other businesses, the various media outlets are diverse. You may have heard horror stories about reporters who ruin crime scenes and broadcast erroneous stories in their rush to be the first to get the news story out. This is not always the case, but you must be able to respond to the potential damage reporters can cause. Having a carefully thought out and well-documented media coverage plan in place will facilitate better coordination with the press. Contrary to the beliefs of many, the media can be of tremendous assistance following a crisis.

An employee must be designated to handle all media contacts. This person and a designated backup person should be identified in the response plan so there is no question as to whom the media should be referred. The media representative should be granted authority to make statements to the media without asking permission from higher up. Things happen fast, and a quick response is needed. Because this designated employee will represent the company to the community and possibly to a much larger audience, he or she should be skilled in public relations and speaking. Forms can be designed to help coordinate facts and details to assist in the communication process.

Other employees should be instructed not to talk to the media immediately after a tragic incident. Most employees have not had much experience dealing with the media. They may try to accommodate media questions out of courtesy and the desire to help. However, they will not know all the facts of the incident, and misinformed employees can easily, and unintentionally, provide statements based on hearsay or lies that will cause harm to coworkers, their families, and the company. As part of their training program, employees should be told in advance to whom they should refer reporters.

When dealing with the media, the company's spokesperson should provide only the facts, not opinion. The spokesperson's opinion may not be that of the company or the other employees. Care must also be exercised not to make assumptions or provide details that might later be used in litigation. If the suspect is an employee or former employee, do not discuss particulars about his or her work history, especially on performance related issues.

Most reporters will cooperate fully with the company's spokesperson. This being the case, the spokesperson should feel free to ask reporters to be patient in waiting for the details. When reporters believe that the spokesperson is being up-front and honest with them, they will be more understanding of the needs of the company.

Rarely is a "no comment" statement in the best interests of the company. Reporters are there to get the story, and if the story does not come from the company spokesperson, they will look elsewhere for their information. They might question employees, neighbors, and even the patron of the local bar and grill.

A press statement can be a good tool for informing employees of what is expected of them. Large businesses are usually not able to call every employee in a timely and effective manner. When the business is small, all employees should be notified by telephone.

The company spokesperson can help guarantee that employees are provided with factual information through press releases. Information on the business being closed, modified hours of service, or the movement of business operations to an alternative site can be passed along in this manner.

Media Coverage

- After a violent incident has occurred, things will be extremely chaotic.

- Reporters will be everywhere.

- Information in the first hours after the incident will, at best, be scarce and incomplete. You will not know the answers to all of the media's questions.

- An employee should be designated in advance to handle media contact.

- Other employees should be told in advance not to respond to media questions.

- Full cooperation with the media should be attempted. The media can be of tremendous assistance in communicating with employees, customers, and the community.

- Rarely is a "no comment" statement in the best interests of the company. What the media (and employees) don't know, they might make up or speculate.

John's Story

In 1994, twenty-five-year-old John got the Christmas gift of a lifetime. Actually, John received the gift of life. Like a cat that has multiple lives, John, too, began a second life. John spent Christmas Day heavily sedated in a hospital in New York as he recovered from numerous surgeries. The ordeal started on the evening of December 20 at approximately 8:20 during a robbery in the store where John worked.

A year earlier, John had graduated from Slippery Rock University in Pennsylvania and was offered a position as assistant manager in a clothing store in Palymra, New York. At a slim 6'3", John displayed youth and confidence. Life was good, and his future was full of promise.

John moved to New York and began working at the store. He reveled in his position, which offered an abundance of customer contacts. John loved people, and this was his opportunity to do what he loved best. He was proud of his ability to talk to even the rudest customer and have them walk away smiling. Going to work was a pleasure.

On December 20 at 2:00 in the afternoon, John began working his ten-hour shift. The Christmas season was the busiest time for the store, and there were plenty of customers who needed attention. Later that evening, a man walked in and changed John's life forever.

As John was working, the man walked up to him and opened his long coat far enough for John to see at least two guns hidden underneath. The man demanded that John take him to the room where the safe was located. John described the robber as a very old looking forty-five to fifty-year-old white man.

John did as he was told. He walked to the room and fumbled with his keys as he tried to open the locked door. After they went inside the room, the robber took out one of the guns and started hitting John in the face and head. The robber kept talking during the entire incident, saying things like, "I'm going to kill you". John was ordered to open the safe. As he tried to do this, the man kept beating him with the gun. John filled the gym bag with the day's receipts and did not offer any resistance. Store policy was to never resist during a robbery.

The man ordered John to take him to the door located in the rear of the store. To do this, John had to walk back into the merchandise area of the store where approximately two hundred customers were shopping.

During the walk to the back door, another employee called to John for assistance with a customer in the layaway department. John said he would be back in a minute to help. He didn't want to attract any attention that might endanger other employees or customers inside the store. During the entire time, the robber kept the gun tight against John's back.

Once outside the customers' view in the back of the store, the robber ordered John to run to the door. Again, John offered no resistance. At the back door, the robber pointed the gun, later found to be a nine-millimeter semiautomatic, at John's head. John remembers the man saying something like, "I told you before that I was going to kill you. Now I'm going to do it." The man hit John in the head again. The force of the blow forced John to close his eyes.

John heard a blast and immediately felt what he describes at the worst pain in his life. John does not remember if he lost consciousness or not, but he was suddenly on the floor. Blood was everywhere and the robber was gone.

He tried to get up, but he was dazed and in severe pain. When he did stand up, the floor was slippery from his blood and he fell a second time. He got up again, and this time he made it through the door that separated him from the merchandise area of the store. He might have heard talking or yelling at the time; he really can't remember.

He does remember the blood squirting and gurgling out of his chest. His blood had soaked his hair and was dripping onto his face. He wondered if he had been shot in the head. He wondered if he was going to die. He wondered if the robber had reentered the store and shot customers or other employees.

A nurse, who happened to be shopping in the store at the time, came running. She quickly started administering first aid while others called for the police and an ambulance. For John, the moments that followed were blurry. He may have faded in and out of consciousness in the store and in the ambulance. He remembers feeling total disbelief at what had happened.

At the hospital, three surgeons were immediately summoned: one to stop the bleeding in the severed blood veins from his chest going into his brain, one to care for the nerves that had been injured, and one to try to reconstruct the bones that had been shattered in his chest.

The next day, a doctor encouraged John to call his parents in Iowa, and let them know what happened. John resisted, not wanting to worry his parents, especially before the holidays. At the doctor's prodding, John did make the call. He doesn't remember much of the call, only telling his parents he had been shot in the chest. His parents arrived shortly thereafter. John does not remember if it was before, after, or on Christmas Day.

Two weeks later John was released from the hospital to begin the long process of trying to reclaim the sanctity of life that he had known only a few weeks earlier. For John and the many victims of workplace violence, it proved impossible. The days of confidence and trust were gone.

The weeks and months that followed were filled with pain and despair. Family and friends tried to bridge the breach that now filled John's life, but John resisted. As with many other crime victims, John suffered emotional injuries as well as physical injuries. John was robbed of more than money in the safe that night. His poise and self-assurance were gone.

Physically unable to work, John spent the next four months finding solace in alcohol and self-destruction. He played "Russian roulette" with his motorcycle, unconsciously wishing for death. He no longer cared about the things he used to care about. He became abusive. His relationship with his girlfriend deteriorated and eventually ended.

John suffered violent rages. He hit friends for the first time in his life. He no longer answered the telephone or returned calls. Executives from the company tried many times to make contact with the injured employee. Their calls were ignored. John left his home only for doctors' visits and to buy tequila and other liquor. John's religious beliefs were damaged.

This behavior continued for months before a nurse finally convinced John to see a counselor. Knowing the severity of his recent actions, John agreed. Based on his behavior and symptoms, the diagnosis was quick: John was suffering from severe depression and post-traumatic stress disorder.

Five months after the incident occurred, John started attending weekly counseling. It took another five months for John to start feeling like he had a future again. John was able to reconcile with his girlfriend and they eventually became engaged.

John still feels fear at the thought of walking down neighborhood streets. He still hates the thought of losing control of himself and the possibility of being victimized by another criminal.

The nine-millimeter bullet still sits in his shoulder. The nerve damage has not healed and his left arm is still numb, but John is starting to talk about going back to work again. During the interview, John made it perfectly clear that he believes that the clothing store chain where he worked is a great company to work for and that management really cares about the employees. John is quite satisfied with the company, but for his next position, he is hoping for an office job that will take him away from the constant face-to-face customer contact that he truly enjoyed before.

POST-TRAUMATIC STRESS

Experiencing a traumatic event can have long-lasting and devastating effects on victims of violent crime. The symptoms associated with the stress range from relatively mild to totally disabling, depending on a multitude of factors characteristic of both the victim and the circumstances involving the incident.

Before businesses can establish appropriate plans for intervention and therapy, they must understand the nature and causes of post-traumatic stress disorder (PTSD). Employee-assistance programs (EAPs) can be valuable to organizations that are developing business recovery strategies. Other counseling programs can also provide tremendous assistance to employees after a violent or other traumatic incident in the workplace. With advanced planning, the long-term damages of the incident can be managed so as to reduce the impact on the employees and the company.

In an interview, clinical social worker Kenneth Wernimont shed some light on the disabling disorder that individuals may experience as a result of witnessing a traumatic event, such as a violent act or injury in the workplace. The disorder may also appear after other traumatic events that result in a person's feeling that his or her survival, or the survival of a loved one, is in jeopardy. For example, an automobile accident that kills or severely maims people and a tornado or other natural disaster that severely damages a person's livelihood are examples of nonviolent events that may trigger PTSD.

Post-traumatic stress disorder differs from temporary post-traumatic stress. When a person is still symptomatic a month after the incident, professional psychological help is needed for the victim to recover.

Wernimont has over thirty years of experience in clinical social work in the mental health field and has treated a number of patients affected by PTSD. He says this type of diagnosis is relatively new to the field of mental health. Only a few years ago, a patient suffering from PTSD might have been given another diagnosis. The more accurate diagnosis of PTSD can be useful in identifying and treating victims who have witnessed or otherwise experienced a violent or traumatic event.

People who suffer from post-traumatic stress experience a variety of symptoms. They often experience recurring dreams about the incident. Although they may not relive the exact set of circumstances in the nightmare, the feelings experienced during the incident will be present. The emotions in the dream may be symbolic of great levels of anxiety, fear, loss, and, in some circumstances, guilt.

The distress that the victims felt at the time of the incident commonly recurs. They may say that they are unable to shake an unpleasant feeling. For some, the recurring feelings may only surface when they come into contact with a stimulus that reminds them of the trauma. A prime example of this would be a person who had a car accident that killed members of his or her family. The person may appear to be okay in most respects, but may experience overwhelming distress whenever attempting to drive a car. For other victims, the distress only occurs around the anniversary of the incident.

Flashbacks are another possible symptom of post-traumatic stress. This symptom is frequently documented among veterans. In a flashback, the victim actually acts and feels as if he or she is reliving the experience.

According to Wernimont, "the intensity of the reactions to traumatic events can in some ways, but not entirely, be predicted based on previous experiences." Wernimont postulates that patients suffering from post-traumatic stress disorder may have faced other traumatic events earlier in life, possibly as a child or young adult. The patient often does not consciously make the correlation between the events. The victim who has experienced similar events earlier in life will often be more severely traumatized.

"Society as a whole has taught individuals to suppress feelings," Wernimont says. "As a child, we are taught to quit crying, hush up, and not talk about dirty laundry." Later in life, peer pressure dictates the amounts of tolerance individuals are afforded when recovering from stressful events. After the death of a loved one, there comes a time when friends, family, and coworkers tell the bereaved to get on with life. The grieving person is prompted to stop showing emotion. Unfortunately, in most cases this is exactly what happens.

When the victim of a traumatic event fails to deal with its emotional impact, it becomes buried but never goes away. The occurrence of a second event that produces a similar emotional impact can unleash the trauma concealed from the first event. As a result, the victim now has two tragedies to deal with.

Keeping emotions buried requires energy, resulting in less energy to focus on the more productive aspects of life. An increase in overall levels of anxiety, tension, and irritability is another byproduct of trying to keep emotions hidden. The individual's overall well-being is diminished.

Wernimont believes that people can become so conditioned in covering up pain and suffering that they begin to automatically suppress distressing feelings without the aid of external forces. "This is one of the reasons EAP services should be available immediately following a traumatic incident," Wernimont says. "The mental health professionals will allow the traumatized employees the opportunity to express their feelings as well as provide the tools needed to begin to process their feelings before they have the chance to bury them. EAPs will give the employees the information they need right away." Some people may even need to be granted permission to cry.

"The body has built-in defense and survival mechanisms, such as adrenaline surges, that allow an individual who is experiencing imminent, severe, and traumatic events to block the immediate feelings the body is experiencing," Wernimont says. "This reaction is common among those experiencing violent acts. This form of denial blocks the emotional impact of the trauma and allows the person to continue in the face of great trauma."

Feelings of detachment also can be systematic of post-traumatic stress disorder. Victims may lose interest in friends and family and become alienated from loved ones. They may isolate themselves emotionally.

Employees who fail to recover from the trauma will seclude themselves from their coworkers, often eating alone and working in silence.

Victims may feel and live as if there is no tomorrow. Their plans may become shortsighted, and their future may appear bleak to them. Employees who once talked a great deal about having children may forgo their plans. They may put career-advancement opportunities on hold. Long-term plans, such as obtaining a college degree or buying a house, may be laid by the wayside.

Addictive tendencies (such as addiction to alcohol, drugs, food, or shopping) can develop. These tendencies may be expressed in alcohol or drug abuse as well as a wide range of other obsessive-compulsive behaviors, such as eating disorders.

Post-traumatic denial is common and can be expressed in several forms. Victims may deny the incident ever took place. They may have amnesia regarding the entire incident or certain aspects of the incident. They may go to great lengths to avoid any stimuli associated with the incident. If the trauma was a car accident, for example, the victim may go far out of her way to avoid driving by the accident site. Traumatized employees might avoid the company cafeteria if the cafeteria was the location of the violence.

Victims who are seemingly able to deny the emotional impact of a traumatic incident are setting themselves at risk for the future. Just as a second traumatic event unleashes the impact of the first, these people are walking around with an emotional bomb inside them. It might be weeks, months, or even years later that they encounter a stimulus causing the denied feelings to emerge.

Imagine for a moment that—unknown to you—a coworker is a victim of the classic date rape. She had dated the assailant once or twice before the rape, and she liked and trusted him. After the assault, rather than dealing with the emotional trauma, the victim, who mistakenly feels that she is partly to blame, suppresses her feelings in the form of denial.

After a while, she decides to date another man. At the end of the evening, he attempts to kiss her goodnight. She explodes, screaming, yelling, shaking, and crying. What the date didn't have any way of knowing was that he just provided her with the emotional stimulus that exhumed her buried emotional trauma.

This type of situation can happen very innocently when dealing with employees on various other issues. Suppose that a subordinate of yours had a previous supervisor who degraded and humiliated him daily. When you try to instruct the employee, you may be the recipient of misdirected rage. In this situation, there are no winners. You lose, the employee loses, and the company loses.

Understanding how devastating post-traumatic stress disorder can affect victims of crime clarifies why immediate care is needed for workers who are traumatized in the course of their employment. The longer the employee is allowed to suppress his or her feelings, the longer the employee will require medical treatment later on. No responsible person wants to deny employees treatment and launch them into a life filled with pain and anguish.

Characteristics of Post-Traumatic Stress Disorder (PTSD)

This disorder sometimes occurs after a person has experienced a traumatic event that causes severe stress. Events precipitating PTSD include a threat to the person's life or another person's life, the destruction of the person's home or community by a natural disaster or other event, and witnessing an accident or severe violence in which a person was killed or injured. The following list describes the characteristics associated with PTSD, where the duration of the effects is longer than one month.

I.   The person with PTSD will re-experience the event in at least one of the following manners:

   A. Repeated distressing memories of the event

   B. Recurring distressing dreams of the event

   C. Sudden feelings of reliving the event, such as flashbacks, illusions, or hallucinations

   D. Recurring distress from events that symbolize the traumatic event, including the anniversary of the event

II. The person experiencing PTSD will avoid stimuli associated with the trauma by at least three of the following ways:

   A. Avoiding thoughts or feelings associated with the traumatic event

    B. Avoiding activities that might arouse recollections of the event

    C. Experiencing the inability to recall aspects of the event

    D. Viewing with decreased interest significant events in his or her life

    E. Experiencing feelings of detachment or estrangement from others

    F. Experiencing a restricted range of affect (i.e., a reduced ability to experience emotions)

    G. Experiencing the sense of a shortened future.

III. The person experiencing PTSD will exhibit persistent symptoms of increased arousal characterized by at least two of the following:

    A. Difficulty falling asleep or staying asleep

    B. Outbursts of anger or irritability

    C. Difficulty concentrating

    D. Hyper vigilance

    E. Exaggerated startle response

    F. Reactivity to events that symbolize or represent an aspect of the trauma

Resuming Operations

There comes a time when the business must resume normal operations. The good of the company, its employees, the community, and the stockholders depends on the business again fulfilling the needs of its customers. "Business as usual" will never exist again. Those who have been affected by the violence will never be the same again. Customers and people in the community may never view the business in the same manner again. Key people within the organization may be lost, and the company may need to find replacements for them. Management may falter and stumble as it tries to provide leadership and direction to the wounded company. Times will not be easy for a long time to come. Knowing this, expectations and goals should be modified to allow a gradual return to some form of normality.

With any type of recovery plan, the responsible individuals and their backups must be clearly defined. They must have the authority to make decisions without going through a sea of red tape for approvals. Things will happen quickly, and the decision-makers must be able to respond quickly.

Typically, the owners, executive vice president, chief executive officer, or other top official of the business is placed at the highest level of responsibility to ensure the recovery plan is carried out. The managers of security, facilities, human resources, and public relations also have a significant share in the responsibility.

The security manager is responsible for ensuring security for the building and the employees. Immediately following an incident of violence, security services will be needed to control the crime scene until law enforcement officials take over. Security personnel will also be needed to assist with first aid and the coordination of emergency services. Witnesses will need to be located and taken to secure areas to wait for law enforcement officials to interview them.

After the incident, security services will most likely need to be bolstered. In the hours and days immediately following the violent act, additional security officers may be required to ensure that access-control measures are enforced. Reporters, sightseers, employees, their families, and even the neighborhood kids may try to gain access to the facility or the grounds. In general, do not allow access to anybody who does not have a legitimate reason to be there.

After business operations resume, the presence of security services and additional security measures will be comforting to surviving employees. As employees return to work, they need to feel some level of security in their surroundings. They might also demand extra security measures be established before they return to work.

The security manager will also need to investigate the incident. Additional security policies and procedures will likely be required, and the security and human resources managers must be able to respond to. those needs quickly. The security audit should be reviewed to ensure compliance with all security issues.

The facilities manager coordinates the cleaning up of the site. The services of the maintenance department or an external vendor will be needed to repair the building if damage was done. Bullet holes must be filled and painted, drywall replaced as needed. Any blood must be cleaned up. Consideration should be given in advance to selecting vendors with experience with blood-borne pathogen standards.

Broken windows and furniture must be removed or repaired. Carpeting may need to be replaced. When employees return to work, they should not be subjected to gruesome reminders of the incident. In one incident at a post office, the returning employees were shocked to see bullet holes that had not been repaired in the walls.

Human resources personnel have a vital role in the recovery process. Their actions immediately following the incident and in the days, weeks, and months ahead determine whether the organization will survive. Employees are the company's biggest asset, and after a traumatic incident, extra care must be used to protect that asset.

An EAP service should be notified immediately after the danger has passed. If the company does not have an existing EAP, one should be selected as part of the recovery program. As a last resort, the telephone book will provide a list of consultant services that might be available at a moment's notice. When a disaster occurs, most people and businesses try to be accommodating, but planning is essential.

The human resources department can assist management in determining when to resume operations. The well-being of the employees and victims, their families, the community, and the business's customers and stockholders must all be taken into consideration.

After incidents of workplace violence, some businesses never reopen. When the McDonald's in National City, California, experienced one of the worst cases of mass killing in the history of the United States, the restaurant was torn down, and a park was rebuilt in its place. McDonald's corporation funded the construction.

Although time is said to heal all wounds, the wounds of the company will never heal if it stays closed for too long. Consumer confidence will deteriorate if operations are suspended for too long. As the old adage goes, the best time to jump back on the horse is as soon as you fall off it. Do not delay reopening the business for too long. You don't want customers to think that the business was permanently closed due to the episode. Customer confidence must be regained for the benefit of your employees, customers, the community, and stockholders.

PART FIVE
THE CALIFORNIA OCCUPATIONAL SAFETY AND HEALTH ADMINISTRATION'S MODEL PROGRAM

CHAPTER TEN

THE CALIFORNIA OCCUPATIONAL SAFETY AND HEALTH ADMINISTRATION ADDRESSES WORKPLACE VIOLENCE

In August 1994, the California Occupational Safety and Health Administration (CAL/OSHA) published a set of safety guidelines designed to prevent workplace violence. These guidelines were published after it became apparent that workplace violence was a very serious threat to the safety and well being of employees in the state. The guidelines encompass a range of security concerns, from robbery prevention to self-audit procedures.

Development of the guidelines began at a conference on workplace security in Los Angels in April 1994. An advisory committee was formed to examine the issue of workplace violence in California and to explore techniques for preventing it. During the April conference, "many advisory committee participants commented that the idea of developing a standard specific to workplace security and emergency action plans should be actively explored."[1]

Since then, CAL/OSHA has drafted a model Injury and Illness Prevention Program for Workplace Security (reproduced at the end of this chapter). The model program is unique for a couple of reasons. First, it brings together the fields of safety and security. The Occupational Health and Safety Administration (OSHA) offices, including CAL/OSHA, have typically addressed safety issues in the workplace, but not security. Although OSHA has had the legal authority to issue citations for security issues that constitute a hazard for employees under the General Duty Clause, it usually focuses on health and safety hazards resulting from hazardous work and conditions.

Another interesting aspect of the program is that businesses in California are not currently required by CAL/OSHA to follow the program. A footer is included on every page of the model program advising readers that compliance is not required, but that when hazards do exist, the reader may want to use all or parts of the model.

This statement is, in ways, deceiving. Business owners who ignore the recommendations because they believe that the model does not pertain to them need to reconsider. OSHA's General Duty Clause states that employers must provide their employees with a safe work environment free of known hazards. When a business recognizes that a safety hazard does exist and fails to correct the hazard, it could be cited under the General Duty Clause. OSHA recognizes the risks associated with violent crimes as safety hazards. In addition, OSHA's regulations are only a small part of the regulatory environment surrounding security issues. Failure to fix a recognized hazard could prove costly if a lawsuit is filed charging the employer with negligence. So, although OSHA may not specifically require businesses to comply with it's security standards, the business owner and other responsible individuals may be legally responsible for failing to maintain a safe and healthy work environment.

Looking at the statistics presented, it's easy to see why concern prompted CAL/OSHA to act. According to the California Division of Labor Statistics and Research, there were 615 work-related deaths in the United States in 1993. Of the 615 recorded deaths, 230 (36.4 percent) were directly related to assaults and other violent acts, a dramatic increase from 1992. In 1993, violence in the workplace was the leading cause of work-related deaths in California.

The cause of death for the majority of women killed on the job in 1993 was homicide. In that year, 48.2 percent of the women who died on the job were murdered. Robbers, estranged partners, former employees, and customers killed them. Women were more likely to die on the job in an act of violence that from almost all other causes put together.

When we think about the friends and families who are left to mourn these victims' deaths, it's easy to understand the urgency in developing guidelines to prevent occupational violence. Although no one likes to have his or her actions regulated by the government, it should be evident that some kind of action plan is needed to stop the bloodshed.

THINGS TO COME

Just as California's anti-stalking laws started a movement that swept across the country, CAL/OSHA's model workplace security program will likely become part of a national law effecting businesses across the United States. Security and safety managers who want to act now to ensure compliance later should look to the CAL/OSHA model program for insight into what the future might hold.

The is ample reason to believe that CAL/OSHA's model program will become increasingly significant to businesses all across the United States in the years to come. Laws exist today to regulate such trivia as the thickness of pickles served in fast-food restaurants. Compare the significance of pickle thickness to that of workplace violence and other crimes prevalent in today's society. How long will it be before federal laws mandate that all businesses address security issues?

The following is a reproduction of the *CAL/OSHA Model Injury and Illness Prevention Program for Workplace Security.*

INJURY & ILLNESS PREVENTION MODEL PROGRAM FOR WORK-PLACE SECURITY

Revised August, 1995

This publication is not meant to be either a substitute for a legal interpretation of the occupational safety and health standards. The reader is cautioned to refer directly to Title 8 of the California Code of Regulations for detailed and exact information, specifications, and exceptions.

WHO SHOULD USE THIS MODEL PROGRAM?

NO ONE IS REQUIRED TO USE THIS MODEL PROGRAM.

However, if you determine that workplace security hazards exist in your workplace, you may want to use some or all of this Model Program or develop your own program independently.

Many workplaces are at risk for workplace violence, but certain workplaces are recognized to be at significantly greater risk than others. Therefore, every employer should perform an initial assessment to identify workplace security issues. If the initial assessment determines that workers are at a significant risk for workplace violence then the employer should review the material presented in this Model Program.

There are a number of factors that have been shown to contribute to the risk of violence in the workplace. If you have one or more of the following factors at your workplace, then you should consider your workplace to be at potential risk of violence:

- Exchange of money.

- Working alone at night and during early morning hours.

- Availability of valued items, e.g., money and jewelry.

- Guarding money or valuable property or possessions.

- Performing public safety functions in the community.

- Working with patients, clients, customers, or students known or suspected to have a history of violence.

- Workers with a history of assaults or who exhibit belligerent, intimidating, and threatening behavior to others.

These are just some of the major factors that contribute to workplace violence. If you have identified any of these, or other indicators of violence in the workplace, then a further evaluation should be performed.

WORKPLACE VIOLENCE IN CALIFORNIA

The circumstances associated with workplace violence in California can be divided into three major types. However, it is important to keep in mind that a particular occupation or workplace may be subject to more than one type.

Type I – In California, the majority of fatal workplace assaults involve a person entering a small late-night retail establishment, e.g., liquor store, gas station, or a convenience food store, to commit a robbery. During the commission of the robbery, an employee, or more likely, the proprietor, is killed or injured.

Workers or proprietors who have face-to-face contact and exchange money with the public, who work late at night and into the early morning hours, and who often work alone or in very small numbers are at greatest risk of a Type I event. While the assailant may feign being a customer as a pretext to enter the establishment, he or she has no legitimate relationship to the workplace.

Retail robberies resulting in workplace assaults usually occur between the late night and early morning hours and are most often armed robberies. In addition to workers who are classified as cashiers, many victims of late night retail violence are supervisors or proprietors who are attacked while locking up their establishment for the night, or janitors who are assaulted while cleaning the establishment after it is closed.

Other occupations/workplaces may be at risk of a Type I event. For instance, assaults on taxicab drivers also involve a pattern similar to retail robberies. The attack is likely to involve an assailant pretending to be a bona fide passenger during the late night or early morning hours who enters the taxicab to rob the driver of his or her fare receipts. Type I events also involve assaults on security guards. It has been known for sometime that security guards are at risk of assault when protecting valuable property that is the object of an armed robbery.

Type II – A Type II workplace violence event involves an assault or threat by someone who is either the recipient or the object of a service provided by the affected workplace or the victim. Type II events involve fatal or nonfatal injuries to individuals who provide services to the public. These events chiefly involve assaults on public safety and correctional personnel, municipal bus or railway drivers, health care and social service providers, teachers, sales personnel, and other public or private service sector workers who provide professional, public safety, administrative, or business services to the public.

Law enforcement personnel are at risk of assault from the "object" of public safety services (suspicious persons, detainees, or arrestees) when making arrests, conducting drug raids, responding to calls involving robberies or domestic disputes, serving warrants and eviction notices, and investigating suspicious vehicles. Similarly, correctional personnel are at risk of assault while guarding and transporting jail or prison inmates.

Of increasing concern, though, are Type II events involving assaults to the following types of service providers:

(1) Medical care providers in acute care hospitals, long-term care facilities, outpatient clinics, and home health agencies;

(2) Mental health and psychiatric care providers in inpatient facilities, outpatient clinics, residential sites, and home health agencies;

(3) Alcohol and drug treatment providers;

(4) Social welfare providers in unemployment offices, welfare eligibility offices, homeless shelters, probation offices, and child welfare agencies;

(5) Teaching, administrative, and support staff in schools where students have a history of violent behavior; and

(6) Other types of service providers, e.g., justice system personnel, customer service representatives, and delivery personnel.

Unlike Type I events which often represent irregular occurrences in the life of any particular at-risk establishment, Type II events occur on a daily basis in many service establishments, and therefore represent a more pervasive risk for many service providers.

Type III – A Type III workplace violence event consists of an assault by an individual who has some employment-related involvement with the workplace. A Type III event usually involves a threat of violence, or a physical act of violence resulting in a fatal or nonfatal injury, by a current or former worker, supervisor or manager; a current or former spouse or lover; a relative or friend; or some other person who has a dispute involving an worker of the workplace.

Available data indicates that a Type III event is not associated with a specific type of workplace or occupation. Any workplace can be at risk of a Type III event. However, Type III events account for a much smaller proportion of fatal workplace injuries than Types I and II. Nevertheless, Type III fatalities often attract significant media attention and are perceived as much more common than they actually are.

INJURY AND ILLNESS PREVENTION PROGRAM FOR WORKPLACE SECURITY

Our establishment's Injury and Illness Prevention (IIP) Program for Workplace Security addresses the hazards known to be associated with the three major types of workplace violence. Type I workplace violence involves a violent act by an assailant with no legitimate relationship to the workplace who enters the workplace to commit a robbery or other criminal act. Type II involves a violent act or threat of violence by a recipient of a service provided by our establishment, such as a client, patient, customer, passenger, or a criminal suspect or prisoner. Type III involves a violent act or threat of violence by a current or former worker, supervisor, or manager, or another person who has some employment-related involvement with our establishment, such as a worker's spouse or lover, a worker's relative or friend, or another person who has a dispute with one of our workers.

NOTE: No one is required to use this Model Program. However, if you determine that workplace security hazards exist in your workplace, you may want to use some or all of this Model Program or develop your own program independently.

RESPONSIBILITY

We have decided to assign responsibility for security in our workplace. The IIP Program administrator for workplace security is_____and has the authority and responsibility for implementing the provisions of this program for_____.

All managers and supervisors are responsible for implementing and maintaining this IIP Program in their work areas and for answering worker questions about the IIP Program. A copy of this IIP Program is available from each manager and supervisor.

COMPLIANCE

We have established the following policy to ensure compliance with our rules on workplace security.

Management of our establishment is committed to ensuring that all safety and health policies and procedures involving workplace security are clearly communicated and understood by all workers.

All workers are responsible for using safe work practices, for following all directives, policies, and procedures, and for assisting in maintaining a safe and secure work environment. Our system of ensuring that all workers, including supervisors and managers, comply with work practices that are designed to make the workplace more secure, and do not engage in threats or physical actions which create a security hazard for others in the workplace, include:

- Informing workers, supervisors, and managers of the provisions of our IIP Program for Workplace Security.

- Evaluating the performance of all workers in complying with our establishment's workplace security measures.

- Recognizing workers who perform work practices which promote security in the workplace.

- Providing training and/or counseling to workers whose performance is deficient in complying with work practices designed to ensure workplace security.

- Disciplining workers for failure to comply with workplace security practices.

- The following practices that ensure worker compliance with workplace security directives, policies, and procedures:

NOTE: No one is required to use this Model Program. However, if you determine that workplace security hazards exist in your workplace, you may want to use some or all or part of this Model Program or develop your own program independently.

COMMUNICATION

At our establishment, we recognize that to maintain a safe, healthy, and secure workplace we must have open, two-way communication between all workers, including managers and supervisors, on all workplace safety, health, and security issues. Our establishment has a communication system designed to encourage a continuous flow of safety, health, and security information between management and our workers without fear of reprisal and in a form that is readily understandable. Our communication system consists of the following checked items:

- New worker orientation on our establishment's workplace security policies, procedures, and work practices.

- Periodic review of our IIP Program for Workplace Security with all personnel.

- Training programs designed to address specific aspects of workplace security unique to our establishment.

- Regularly scheduled safety meetings with all personnel that include workplace security discussions.

- A system to ensure that all workers, including managers and supervisors, understand the workplace security policies.

- Posted or distributed workplace security information.

- A system for workers to inform management about workplace security hazards or threats of violence.

- Procedures for protecting workers who report threats from retaliation by the person making the threats.

- Addressing security issues at our workplace security team meetings.

- Our establishment has fewer than ten workers and communicates with and instructs workers orally about general safe work practices with respect to workplace security.

- Other:_____
  _____
  _____

NOTE: No one is required to use this Model Program. However, if you determine that workplace security hazards exist in your workplace, you may want to use some or all of this Model Program or develop your own program independently.

HAZARD ASSESSMENT

We will be performing workplace hazard assessment for workplace security in the form of periodic inspections. Periodic inspections to identify and evaluate workplace security hazards and threats of workplace violence are performed by the following observer(s) in the following areas of our workplace:

Observer Area

Periodic inspections are performed according to the following schedule:
_____;

Frequency (daily, weekly, monthly, etc.)

- When we initially established our IIP Program for Workplace Security;

- When new, previously unidentified security hazards are recognized;

- When occupational injuries or threats of injury occur; and

- Whenever workplace security conditions warrant an inspection.

Periodic inspections for security hazards consist of identification and evaluation of workplace security hazards and changes in worker work practices, and may require assessing for more than one type of workplace violence. Our establishment performs inspections for each type of workplace violence by using the methods specified below to identify and evaluate workplace security hazards.

Inspections for Type I workplace security hazards include assessing:

- The exterior and interior of the workplace for its attractiveness to robbers.

- The need for security surveillance measures, such as mirrors or cameras.

- Posting of signs notifying the public that limited cash is kept on the premises.

- Procedures for worker response during a robbery or other criminal act.

- Procedures for reporting suspicious persons or activities.

- Posting of emergency telephone numbers for law enforcement, fire, and medical services where workers have access to a telephone with an outside line.

- Limiting the amount of cash on hand and using time access safes for large bills.

- Other: _____
  _____
  _____

NOTE: No one is required to use this Model Program. However, if you determine that workplace security hazards exist in your workplace, you may want to use some or all of this Model Program or develop your own program independently.

Inspections for Type II workplace security hazards include assessing:

Access to, and freedom of movement within, the workplace.

Adequacy of workplace security systems, such as door locks, security windows, physical barriers, and restraint systems.

Frequency and severity of threatening or hostile situations that may lead to violent acts by persons who are service recipients of our establishment.

Workers skill in safely handling threatening or hostile service recipients.

Effectiveness of systems and procedures to warn others of a security danger or to summon assistance, e.g., alarms or panic buttons.

The use of work practices such as "buddy" systems for specified emergency events.

The availability of worker escape routes.

Other: _____
_____
_____

Inspections for Type III workplace security hazards include assessing:

- How well our establishment's anti-violence policy has been communicated to workers, supervisors, or managers.

- How well our establishment's management and workers communicate with each other.

- Our workers', supervisors', and managers' knowledge of the warning signs of potential workplace violence.

- Access to, and freedom of movement within, the workplace by non-workers, including recently discharged workers or persons with whom one of our worker's is having a dispute.

- Frequency and severity of worker reports of threats of physical or verbal abuse by managers, supervisors, or other workers.

- Any prior violent acts, threats of physical violence, verbal abuse, property damage, or other signs of strain or pressure in the workplace.

- Worker disciplinary and discharge procedures.

- Other:_____

_____

NOTE: No one is required to use this Model Program. However, if you determine that workplace security hazards exist in your workplace, you may want to use some or all of this Model Program or develop your own program independently.

INCIDENT INVESTIGATIONS

We have established the following policy for investigating incidents of workplace violence.

Our procedures for investigating incidents of workplace violence, which includes threats and physical injury, include:

- Reviewing all previous incidents.

- Visiting the scene of an incident as soon as possible.

- Interviewing threatened or injured workers and witnesses.

- Examining the workplace for security risk factors associated with the incident, including any previous reports of inappropriate behavior by the perpetrator.

- Determining the cause of the incident.

- Taking corrective action to prevent the incident from recurring.

- Recording the findings and corrective actions taken.

- Other:_____
  _____

HAZARD CORRECTION

Hazards which threaten the security of workers shall be corrected in a timely manner based on severity when they are first observed or discovered.

Corrective measures for Type I workplace security hazards can include:

- Making the workplace unattractive to robbers.

- Utilizing surveillance measures, such as cameras or mirrors, to provide information as to what is going on outside and inside the workplace.

- Procedures for reporting suspicious persons or activities.

- Posting of emergency telephone numbers for law enforcement, fire, and medical services where workers have access to a telephone with an outside line.

- Posting of signs notifying the public that limited cash is kept on the premises.

- Limiting the amount of cash on hand and using time access safes for large bills.

- Worker, supervisor, and management training on emergency action procedures.

- Other:_____
  _____

NOTE: No one is required to use this Model Program. However, if you determine that workplace security hazards exist in your workplace, you may want to use some or all of this Model Program or develop your own program independently.

Corrective measures for Type II workplace security hazards include:

- Controlling access to the workplace and freedom of movement within it, consistent with business necessity.

- Ensuring the adequacy of workplace security systems, such as door locks, security windows, physical barriers, and restraint systems.

- Providing worker training in recognizing and handling threatening or hostile situations that may lead to violent acts by persons who are service recipients of our establishment.

- Placing effective systems to warn others of a security danger or to summon assistance, e.g., alarms or panic buttons.

- Providing procedures for a "buddy" system for specified emergency events.

- Ensuring adequate worker escape routes.

- Other:_____

_____

Corrective measures for Type III workplace security hazards include:

- Effectively communicating our establishment's anti-violence policy to all workers, supervisors, or managers.

- Improving how well our establishment's management and workers communicate with each other.

- Increasing awareness by workers, supervisors, and managers of the warning signs of potential workplace violence.

- Controlling access to, and freedom of movement within, the workplace by non-workers, including recently discharged workers or persons with whom one of our worker's is having a dispute.

- Providing counseling to workers, supervisors, or managers who exhibit behavior that represents strain or pressure which may lead to physical or verbal abuse of coworkers.

- Ensure that all reports of violent acts, threats of physical violence, verbal abuse, property damage, or other signs of strain or pressure in the workplace are handled effectively by management and that the person making the report is not subject to retaliation by the person making the threat.

- Ensure that worker disciplinary and discharge procedures address the potential for workplace violence.

- Other:_____

_____

NOTE: No one is required to use this Model Program. However, if you determine that workplace security hazards exist in your workplace, you may want to use some or all of this Model Program or develop your own program independently.

TRAINING AND INSTRUCTION

We have established the following policy on training all workers with respect to workplace security.

All workers, including managers and supervisors, shall have training and instruction on general and job-specific workplace security practices. Training and instruction shall be provided when the IIP Program for Workplace Security is first established and periodically thereafter. Training shall also be provided to all new workers and to other workers for whom training has not previously been provided and to all workers, supervisors, and managers given new job assignments for which specific workplace security training for that job assignment has not previously been provided. Additional training and instruction will be provided to all personnel whenever the employer is made aware of new or previously unrecognized security hazards.

- General workplace security training and instruction includes, but is not limited to, the following:

- Explanation of the IIP Program for Workplace Security including measures for reporting any violent acts or threats of violence.

- Recognition of workplace security hazards including the risk factors associated with the three types of workplace violence.

- Measures to prevent workplace violence, including procedures for reporting workplace security hazards or threats to managers and supervisors.

- Ways to defuse hostile or threatening situations.

- Measures to summon others for assistance.

- Worker routes of escape.

- Notification of law enforcement authorities when a criminal act may have occurred.

- Emergency medical care provided in the event of any violent act upon an worker; and

- Post-event trauma counseling for those workers desiring such assistance.

- In addition, we provide specific instructions to all workers regarding workplace security hazards unique to their job assignment, to the extent that such information was not already covered in other training.

NOTE: No one is required to use this Model Program. However, if you determine that workplace security hazards exist in your workplace, you may want to use some or all of this Model Program or develop your own program independently.

We have chosen the following checked items for Type I training and instruction for managers, supervisors, and workers:

- Crime awareness.

- Location and operation of alarm systems.

- Communication procedures.

- Proper work practices for specific workplace activities, occupations, or assignments, such as late night retail sales, taxi-cab driver, or security guard.

- Other:_____
_____

We have chosen the following checked items for Type II training and instruction for managers, supervisors, and workers:

- Self-protection.

- Dealing with angry, hostile, or threatening individuals.

- Location, operation, care, and maintenance of alarm systems and other protective devices.

- Communication procedures.

- Determination of when to use the "buddy" system or other assistance from coworkers.

- Awareness of indicators that lead to violent acts by service recipients.

- Other:_____
  _____
  _____

We have chosen the following checked items for Type III training and instruction for managers, supervisors, and workers:

- Pre-employment screening practices.

- Worker Assistance Programs.

- Awareness of situational indicators that lead to violent acts.

- Managing with respect and consideration for worker well-being.

- Review of anti-violence policy and procedures.

- Other:_____
  _____

NOTE: No one is required to use this Model Program. However, if you determine that workplace security hazards exist in your workplace, you may want to use some or all of this Model Program or develop your own program independently.[2]

RERERENCES

1. *CAL/OSHA Guidelines for Workplace Security* (San Francisco: Department of Industrial Relations, Division of Occupational Safety and Health, August 1994), p. 21

2. *CAL/OSHA Model Injury and Illness Prevention Program for Workplace Security* (San Francisco: Department of Industrial Relations, Division of Occupational Safety and Health, August 24, 1995).

The September 11th tragedy will live in our memories as a day when the most lives ever were lost due to violent acts against employees in the workplace. While terrorism has not been the focus of this book, the fear of violence in the workplace it has invoked has been. The last decade will go down in business history as the decade in which managers became leaders and departments became teams. The book *Who Moved My Cheese* took up residence on millions of bookshelves across the United States. The troubled economy has forced all businesses to re-examine how they do business. This new era of corporate scandal, bankruptcies, troubled employment outlooks, and eroding retirement plans has added to the stresses that contribute to workplace violence.

By proactively addressing and dealing with workplace violence, we can help control it and, in many cases, stop it. We all have a responsibility to ourselves, to our coworkers, and to our employers to prevent violence and the unnecessary loss of life.

Some people see the likelihood of workplace violence as a very remote variable in their lives. They don't believe that violence can or will strike their company or harm a family member or friend; but it can, and it does, every day. Without prevention, intervention, and resolution of key issues, the violence will continue. Pointing fingers, placing blame, and ignoring the issues only feeds the vicious cycle.

Workplace violence is preventable. In almost every case of workplace violence, there was a point in time when something could have been done to prevent the bloodshed. Many of the measures used to decrease violence are preventative by nature. Policies, procedures, training, and employment screening are only a few of the tools that companies can use to prevent violence.

This is your call to action. This book covered many procedures that will help decrease or stop workplace violence. Reading about them alone is not enough. You must take action. You have been handed the knowledge you need. Now it's up to you to use it and make a difference. God bless.

INDEX

Page references followed by t indicate a table
Page references followed by b indicate a box

A

Abnormal behavior, normal *versus*, 9–12

Absenteeism
abused employees and, 29
abusive relationships and, 27
alcohol abuse and, 24
drug abuse and, 24
security staff and, 98
substance abuse and, 44

Abuse. *See also* Alcohol abuse; Drug abuse
employers and abused employees, 28–29
intimidation and threats and, 104

Access control
photo identification badges and, 93–94
physical barriers and, 93
registration logs and, 95–96

Accidents and injuries, signs of drug misuse and, 22b

Acquaintances, occupational homicides and, 9

ADA. *See* Americans with Disabilities Act (ADA)

Addictive tendencies, post-traumatic stress and, 146

Aggravated assaults. *See also* Assaults
number of victimization during 1993-1999, 7t
percentage increase in number from 1983-1992, 9

Aggressive behavior, dealing with, 104–109

Alarms, panic or duress, 96, 131–132

Alcohol abuse
absenteeism and, 24
economic cost of, 18
as warning sign of violent behavior, 43–44

American Medical Society, domestic violence and, 27

Americans with Disabilities Act (ADA), 4, 79

Angel dust. *See* Phencyclidine

Appearance, drug misuse and, 22b

Application forms, hiring and, 68–70

Armored car services, number of workplace homicides during 1994–1999, 6t

Assaults. *See also* Aggravated assaults
among coworkers, 17
number of victimization during 1993–1999, 7t
number of workers assaulted, 17

Assessment
hazard, 161–164
of signs of potentially violent behavior, 111b
of violent person, 37–38b

Assignment changes, drug misuse and, 21b

Attendance, drug misuse and, 20b

B

Background checks, 72–73
hiring and, 65, 66, 67
Barbiturates, percentage use by
twelfth graders in 1993, 18
Behavior. *See also* Abnormal behavior;
Violent behavior
aggressive or intimidating, dealing
with, 104–109
normal *versus* abnormal types of,
9–12
threatening, 103–111
violent type of, 109–111, 113–132
assessing, 111b
Behavioral interviewing, 71
Body language, threatening behavior
of employees and, 107
Boxer stance, 111
Bureau of Justice Statistics, 2001, 17
Bureau of National Affairs, 27
Business operations, resuming, 148–
150
Business recovery planning, 136–137b

C

California
anti-stalking legislation, 31–32
increase in occupational homicides
in 1992–1993, 9
California Occupational Safety and
Health Administration (CAL/
OSHA), 13
injury and illness prevention model
for workplace security, 155–169
workplace violence, Type I, 14b, 15,
156–157
workplace violence, Type III, 16, 158
workplace violence, Type II, 14b,
15–16, 157–158
workplace violence and, 153–169
CAL/OSHA. *See* California Occupational Safety and Health
Administration (CAL/OSHA)

Cannabis, symptoms of misuse of,
23b
Census of Fatal Occupational Injuries,
number of work-related homicides, 9, 27
Ciechanowski, Arlin, 24–25
Claims (unusual), as warning sign of
violent behavior, 43
Cocaine
money and, 24
percentage use by twelfth graders
in 1993, 18
symptoms of misuse of, 22b
Communications
and access to information, 3
role in securing safe workplace,
160–161
Companies
documenting observations in drug
abuse, 25–26
informing employees about
Employee-assistance programs
(EAPs), 80
internal crimes against, 17–18
losses as a result of domestic
violence, 27
policies and procedures, 55–56
policy statement on workplace
violence, 56b
stalking of employees and, 34
threatening behavior of employees
and policy, 109
Convenience stores
number of robberies in, 124
workplace violence Type I and, 15
Cost, of drug abuse, 18
Crimes
internal, against the company, 17–18
and occupational deaths in 1993, 9
in the United States (1962,1992), 8–9
Crisis intervention team
structure and goals of, 62–63
topics for, 63–64b
training of, 62–63, 64b

D

Denial, post-traumatic stress and, 146

Depressants, symptoms of misuse of, 23b

Detective car services, number of workplace homicides during 1994–1999, 6t

District of Columbia, anti-stalking laws, 32

Distrust and suspicion, 42–43

Diversity in workplace, behavior and, 11

Documentation
of employee behavior in drug abuse, 25–26
intervention and action plans and, 87

Domestic violence
workplace and, 27–31
companies losses as a result of, 27
costs of, 28
evidence of, 29
referral to employee-assistance program, 30–31

Downsizing, 4

DRE. *See* Drug recognition expert (DRE)

Dreams, post-traumatic stress and, 144

Drug abuse
overdose suspicion and, 25
symptoms of, 22–23b
as warning sign of violent behavior, 43–44
in the workplace, 18–26
economic cost of, 18
signs of misuse of, 20–23b
supervisors action with the employee, 25–26
training and, 19

Drug misuse, signs of, 20–23b

Drug recognition expert (DRE), 24

Duress alarms, 96, 131–132

E

EAPs. *See* Employee-assistance programs (EAPs)

Eating and drinking establishments, number of workplace homicides during 1994–1999, 6t

Education
of employees on security and safety, 59–64
as tool to diminish workplace violence, 85

Employee-assistance programs (EAPs), 77–84
clergymen and, 78–79
confidentiality of, 80, 81–82
domestic violence and, 29–30
history of, 77
informing employees of existence of, 80
medical problems and, 81
objectives of, 79
post-traumatic stress and, 143
questions to ask in contracting for, 83–84
referrals to, 29–31, 81
resuming business operations and, 150
role of, 77–78, 79–80
stalking and, 34
timeliness of services of, 80–81
types of, 78

Employees
abused, employers and, 28–29
confronting in drug abuse, 25–26
dealing with threatening behavior of, 103–109
education, topics of, 59–61
homicides and, 5
stalking and, 34
volatile workplace and, 51–55

Employment conditions, violence and, 51–58

Erotomania. *See* Romantic obsession

Escape, violence and, 118–119

External threat management, examples of, 93b

F

Failed relationships, history of, 41–42
Fear, aggressive/intimidating behavior and, 105
Feeling of detachment, post-traumatic stress and, 145
Flashbacks, post-traumatic stress and, 144

G

Gasoline service stations
number of homicides during 1994–1999, 6t
and workplace violence Type I, 15
Grievances, work environment and, 53
Grocery stores, number of homicides during 1994–1999, 6t
Guidelines
of California Occupational Safety and Health Administration on workplace violence, 153
to survive in robbery, 127–128

H

Hallucinogens
percentage use by twelfth graders in 1993, 18
symptoms of misuse of, 23b
Harassment, history of, 46–47
Hazard assessment, 161–164
Hazard correction, 165–167
Heroin, percentage use by twelfth graders in 1993, 18
Hiring, 65–67
background check and, 66
negligent hiring practice and, 57–58, 66

practices for good, 67–68b
special considerations, 67
Homicides
death on the job and, 9
and employees, 5
number for selected industries during 1994–1999, 6t
number of victimization during1993–1999, 7t
occupations with highest rates of, 5

I

Inhalants, symptoms of misuse of, 23b
In-houses services, EAPs and, 78
Injuries and accidents, signs of drug misuse and, 22b
Injury and illness prevention program
model for workplace security, 155–158
for workplace security, 158–159
Internal threat management, examples of, 93b
Intervention and action plans, 84–90
documentation and, 87
initial notice of problem, 84–85
interviewing and, 86–89
investigations of claims, 85
threats and, 87–88
timely reaction to claims and, 85
Interviewing
hiring and, 70–72
intervention and action plans and, 86–89
Intimidating behavior, dealing with, 104–109
Intimidation
history of, 46–47
and threats, 104–105
Investigations, incident, 164–165

J

Job applications, 5, 65

K

Kids and drugs, 24

L

Law enforcement
    rates of victimization in the
        workplace, 6t
    recommendations to decrease risk
        during robbery, 127–128
    workplace violence Type II and, 15
Layoffs
    changes in workplace and, 4
    distrust and suspicion and, 43
Legal aspects, secure work environ-
    ment and, 57–58
Lighting and security, 97
Liquor stores
    number of robberies in, 124
    workplace violence Type I and, 15

M

Manager training
    threats and, 61–62
    topics for, 64b
Marijuana
    percentage use by twelfth graders
        in 1992, 18
    use by males, 25
Media coverage
    after violent crime, 137–143
    celebrity stalking and, 33
    of murder, 10
    workplace violence Type II and, 16
Medical field, rates of victimization in
    the workplace, 6t
Mental health field, rates of victimiza-
    tion in the workplace, 6t
Mood changes, drug misuse and, 21b
Motivations for violence, 13–17
Murder
        of co-worker, 9

increase in number from 1983–
    1992, 9

N

Narcotics, symptoms of misuse of,
    23b
National Census of Fatal Occupational
    Injuries, 5
National Crime Victimization Survey
    of Violent Crime Trends, 7t, 17
National Institute for Occupational
    Safety and Health (NIOSH),
    incident rates calculation, 5
National Rifle Association (NRA), 44
NIOSH. See National Institute for
    Occupational Safety and Health
    (NIOSH)
Noncocaine stimulants, symptoms of
    misuse of, 23b
Normal behavior, abnormal versus, 9–
    12
Northwestern National Life Insurance
    Company Survey, 19
NRA. See National Rifle Association
    (NRA)

O

Occupational deaths
and robbery in 1993, 9
workplace violence Type II and, 15–16
Occupational Health and Safety. See
    also California Occupational
    Safety and Health Administration
    (CAL/OSHA)
    death in the workplace and, 57
Occupational violence
    occupations with highest rates of, 5
    and rates of victimization, 6t
Occupations, high risk, 5–8
Omnibus Employee Testing Act, 19

P

Panic alarms. *See* Duress alarms
PCP, 25
Performance, drug and alcohol abuse
    and, 20, 24
Phencyclidine, symptoms of misuse
    of, 23b
Photo identification badges, access
    control and, 93–94
Physical security, 96–97
Planning
    of business recovery, 136–137b
    post incident, violence and, 135–136
    the termination of employees, 74
Police protection, number of
    workplace homicides during
    1994–1999, 6t
Policies and procedures, 65–100. *See
    also* Companies
    corporate type of, 55–56
Policy statement (sample), workplace
    violence and, 56b
Post incident planning, 135–137
Post office. *See* United States Postal
    Service
Post-traumatic stress, 143–150
Post-traumatic stress disorder (PTSD),
    143
    characteristics of, 147–148
    symptoms of, 144–14
    temporary post-traumatic stress
    and, 144
Productivity, drug misuse and, 21b
Profile of violent person, 37
PTSD. *See* Post-traumatic stress
    disorder (PTSD)
Purchased services, EAPs and, 78

Q

Quality of work, drug misuse and, 21b

R

Rape
    among coworkers, 17
    number of victimization during
    1993–1999, 7t
    numbers from 1983–1992, 9
Recovery strategies, and violent event,
    135–137
Registration log, 95–96
Relationships
    domestic violence and, 28
    drug misuse and, 22b
    failed, history of violence and, 41–42
Relocation, 4
Repeated stalking, definition of, 32
Resume, hiring and the, 68–70
Retail sales, rates of victimization in
    the workplace, 6t
Retail trades, number of homicides
    during 1994-1999, 6t
Rightsizing, 4
Risk factors
    workplace violence and, 8
    workplace violence Type I and, 15
    workplace violence Type II and, 15–
    16
Robbery
    deterrence of, 126–127
    guidelines to survive in, 127–128
    increase in number from 1983-
    1992, 9
    key elements of, 123–126
    motivation for, 44
    number of people murdered
    during, 120
    number of victimization during
    1993–1999, 7t
    occupational deaths in 1993 and, 9
    responsibility after, 129–130
    responsibility during, 128
    the surviving of, 127–128
Romantic obsession, stalking and, 34

S

Safes, 97
Security
  equipment, 97
  injury and illness prevention
      program in workplace and,
      158–159
  management, 98
  physical, 96–97
  responsibility for, 159
  training, topics for, 99b
Security procedures, 90–93
  access control and, 93–96
  budget for, 91
  lighting and, 97
  photo identification badges and,
      93–94
  physical type of, 96–97
  registration log and, 95–96
  risk examining and, 91
  risk identification and, 90
  safes and, 97
  signs and warnings, 97
  threat management and, 92, 93b
  threats and, 91–93
  training topics and, 59, 60, 99b
September 11th tragedy, workplace
    violence and, 171
Sexual assault, number of victimiza-
    tion during 1993–1999, 7t
Shoulder-shrug, 111
SHRM. See Society for Human
    Resource Managers (SHRM)
Signs and warnings, posting of, 97
Society for Human Resource
    Managers (SHRM), 13
Stalking, 31–36
  tips for victims of, 35–36b
Standard Industry Classification (SIC)
    Manual, 5
Statistics
  on women killed on the job, 27
  on workplace violence, 8–9

Stimulants, percentage use by twelfth
    graders in 1993, 18
Stress, in the workplace, 12
Stress-related disabilities claims, 53
Substance abuse. See Alcohol abuse;
    Drug abuse
Supervisors training
  on drug abuse, 19
  threats and, 61–62
  topics for, 59, 64b
Suspicion and distrust, 42–43

T

Taxicab, number of workplace
    homicides during 1994–1999 and,
    6t
Teaching, rates of victimization in the
    workplace, 6t
Telephonic services, EAPs and, 78
Termination of employees, 73–76
  action to follow for, 74–75
  emotional response to, 74
  injunction for, 75
  planning the, 74
  practices for, good, 76b
Threatening behavior, 103–111
  intimidation and threats and, 103–
      104
Threats
  categories of, 91–92
  external type of, 92b
  management for, 93b
  internal type of
  management for, 93b
  intervention and action plans for,
      87–88
  intimidation and, 46–47
  management, 92, 93b
  manager training and, 61–62
  security procedures and, 91–93
  supervisors training and, 61–62
  termination and, 75
  types of, 92b
  victims of intimidation and, 103–104

violent person and, 40–41
warning signs of violent behavior
and, 40–41
Training
of crisis intervention team, 62–63,
64b
detecting signs and symptoms of
drug abuse among employees,
19
of employees, topics for, 63b
and instruction in workplace
security, 167–169
of managers, 61–62, 64b
security, topics for, 99b
security department and, 98–99
supervisors, topics for, 59, 61–62,
64b
Tranquilizers
number of prescriptions for, 24–25
percentage use by twelfth graders
in 1993, 18
Transportation field, rates of victimization in the workplace, 6t

U

Uniform Crime Reports, 8–9
United States, number of forcible
rape in (1962,1992), 8–9
United States Department of Justice,
31
United States Department of Labor,
domestic violence and, 31
United States Department of Labor
Census of Fatal Occupational
injuries, 1993
number of people murdered on
the job, 119
United States of Health and Human
Services, 18
United States Postal Service, homicide
rate in, 5
Unusual claims by employees, as
warning signs, 43

V

Verbal abuse in workplace, 17
Victimization in the workplace, rates
by occupational field, 6t
Victims
of intimidation and threats, 103–104
of stalking, tips for, 32, 35–36b (*See
also* Stalking)
of traumatic event, 145–146
Violence. *see also* Workplace violence
destructive acts of, 18
employment conditions and, 51–58
escaping from, 118–119
fascination with, 46
forms of, 13–36
and media coverage, 137–143
motivations for, 13–17
post incident planning and, 135–137
Violence Against Women Act, 31–32
Violent behavior, 113–132
signs of, 109–111
assessing, 111b
warning signs of, 38–40
alcohol and drug abuse and, 43–
44
distrust and suspicion and, 42–43
failed relationships and history
of, 41–42
fascination with workplace
violence and, 46
threats and, 40–41
unusual claims and, 43
weapons ownership and, 44–45
Violent person, 37–47. *See also* Violent
behavior
assessing, 37–38b
profile of, 37
Volatile workplace, ingredients for, 51–
55

W

Weapons
fascination with, 45–46

ownership of, violent behavior and, 44–45
cooling-off periods for, 44
threatening behavior of employees and, 105–106
Who Moved My Cheese, 171
Women killed on the job, statistics on, 27
Work environment
grievances by employees and, 52–53
secure, legal aspects of, 57–58
Workplace
definition of, 5
diversity behavior in, 11
drug abuse in, 18–26
with highest levels of occupational violence, 5–8
homicide, occupations with, 5
number of victimization in, 7t
signs of drug misuse in, 20–23b
victimization rates in the workplace, 6t

volatile, ingredients for, 51–55
Workplace security
California Occupational Safety and Health Administration, injury and illness prevention model 155–169
ensuring compliance with, 159–160
injury and illness prevention program for, 158–159
role of communications in, 161
training and instruction in, 167–169
Workplace violence
alcohol and drug abuse and, 19
in California, 14b, 156–158
education and, 85
fascination with, 46
numbers on, 9
risk factors and, 8
September 11th tragedy and, 171
types of, major, 14b, 15–17
Work-related homicides, 9

Sandra L. Lanier, CPP, is president of Lanier Security Group, Inc., located in Orlando, Florida. Lanier Security Group specializes in providing security consulting services to Fortune 500 companies and to government entities. Prior to founding Lanier Security Group, Ms. Lanier was the safety and security coordinator at GMAC Mortgage in Waterloo, Iowa, where she was responsible for the research, development, and implementation of corporate-wide education, safety policies, and security management for 122 offices nationwide. She earned a Bachelor of Arts degree in Business Management from Upper Iowa University and an Associates of Arts degree in Police Science from Hawkeye Community College. She attended graduate classes for an MBA at the University of Northern Iowa. Ms. Lanier may be contacted at slanier@lanier-security.com.